AN EXECUTIVE GUIDE TO EMPLOYING CONSULTANTS

❖

AN EXECUTIVE GUIDE TO EMPLOYING CONSULTANTS

❖

Richard E. Zackrison and
Arthur M. Freedman

Gower

Published by
Gower Publishing Limited
Gower House
Croft Road
Aldershot
Hampshire GU11 3HR
England

Gower
131 Main Street
Burlington
Vermont 05401
USA

British Library Cataloguing in Publication Data
Zackrison, Richard E.
    An executive guide to employing consultants
    1. Consultants – Selection and appointment
    I. Title   II. Freedman, Arthur M.
    658.3'11

ISBN 0 566 08271 3

Library of Congress Card Number: 00-102792

Typeset in 10 pt Garamond by IML Typographers, Chester and printed in Great Britain at the University Press, Cambridge.

CONTENTS

❖

LIST OF FIGURES AND TABLES

❖

FIGURES

TABLES

PREFACE

❖

Many years ago one of the authors saw an announcement in a business daily for a two-day 'Consultant Training Course'. Out of curiosity, he registered for the course. In return for a fee of £250 and two days of training he 'learned' that to be successful as a consultant he would need a 'power wardrobe', embossed business cards, an expensive leather attaché case, and someone with a sensual female voice to answer his office telephone. It was also recommended that he seek assignments at least five hundred miles away from his city of residence (the problem of being a prophet in one's own land and all that!).

It's no wonder that so many senior executives and managers distrust people who call themselves 'consultants'. It seems that almost anybody can become a 'consultant' simply by having business cards printed. For example, it is not unusual for retrenched executives, many of whom are on the streets because they were not very effective when they were employed, to hang out a sign promoting their services as 'consultants'.

When we were younger we hoped and believed that incompetent, unethical and/or unprofessional consultants would be revealed and quickly weeded out. Unfortunately, we now realize that such 'consultants' not only survive, but thrive, thanks to an ever expanding market of unsuspecting, naïve and/or desperate potential clients upon which they feed.

As dedicated, professional consultants, we are appalled by indications that 75–80 per cent of all consultant-guided change efforts fall far short of their intended goals and expectations, cost more than the results are worth, cause unexpected and unacceptable side-effects and/or produce results that quickly fade. The unacceptable performance of most change efforts is usually caused by one or more of the following:

1. The effort was ill-advised and should never have been initiated to begin with.

2.   An external consultant was engaged to resolve a problem that should have been dealt with internally, without a consultant.

3.   The consultant did not listen to, appreciate, or attend to the client's expectations, needs and concerns.

4.   An inappropriate type of consultant was engaged for the project.

5.   The consultant was not competent to deal with the problem.

6.   The consultant was not competent to manage the change process.

7.   The effort was begun too late, in that the patient waited until s/he was terminally ill before seeking help.

8.   The management of the client organization was not ready to or capable of managing the change process.

9.   Key members of the organization were unwilling, unprepared or unable to provide adequate support for the change effort.

10.   The results of the consulting effort were inappropriately or ineffectively evaluated or not evaluated at all.

Clearly, incompetent, unqualified, unprofessional consultants are a significant cause of failed change efforts. If management consulting were a true profession there would be set standards of professional and ethical behaviour to ensure that people who claim to be members of that profession are qualified to practice in a professional, competent and ethical manner. Unfortunately, unlike physicians, accountants and attorneys, people who call themselves 'management consultants' do not have to be certified or licensed in order to display a sign. Even when it is widely known in the field that a given consultant is incompetent, unprofessional and/or unethical, fellow consultants do not have the formal power to take away that individual's right to practise.

That means that it is up to you, the client, to cull unprofessional, unethical consultants by hitting them where they are most vulnerable – in their bank accounts. As long as senior managers allow change efforts to be designed, implemented and/or managed by people, internally or externally, who lack the competence, experience and/or commitment necessary to ensure their success, incompetent, unethical and unprofessional consultants will continue to thrive. If ersatz-consultants find that their clients are asking valid questions that they are unable to answer and, as a result, are not getting enough work to survive, we hope that they will be forced to leave the consulting profession.

That is why we wrote this book – to provide senior managers with a set of practical tools that will enable them to distinguish between professional, competent consultants and those who are consultants only by merit of their expensive attaché case, embossed business cards and impressive but meaningless credentials. In writing this book we are well aware that we are likely to upset a number of people, most of whom will be individuals who call themselves 'consultants', but have no right to the title. We will be quite pleased with ourselves if such individuals get angry. It will indicate that we have struck a nerve, threatened their livelihoods or in some way made their lives less comfortable.

The nine chapters of this book are divided into four parts, as follows:

Part I   Identifying the kind of help you need
          Chapter 1   Do you really need a consultant?
          Chapter 2   What type of consultant do you need?

Part II   Building consultant selection criteria
          Chapter 3   Identifying professional, ethical consultants
          Chapter 4   Consultant skills, experience and personal characteristics

Part III Choosing the best consultant for the job
          Chapter 5   Locating prospective consultants
          Chapter 6   Interviewing prospective consultants
          Chapter 7   Evaluating consultant proposals and contracts

Part IV   Managing the consultant project
          Chapter 8   Managing and evaluating consultants
          Chapter 9   Change management

Each part of this book is concluded with a set of checklists designed to help you to apply the ideas presented.*

There are a number of people who have influenced the writing and eventually the publication of this book, including innumerable friends, colleagues and clients. However, there is one person without whose patience and support this book would never have happened – and that is Zack's wife, Sonja. Sonja put up with and nurtured the bodies and egos of two 'madmen' for three weeks in a relatively small cabin along Sweden's Northern Baltic coast. She bolstered up our egos as we sought and dealt with the critical reactions of potential publishers. And, most importantly, she provided unwavering support, energy and enthusiasm for our efforts, despite her own serious health problems.

Now, we invite you to join us as we enter and trek through what we perceive as the 'consultant jungle'. We sincerely hope that you will find your journey beneficial, entertaining and, at times, a bit frightening.

Richard Zackrison
Arthur Freedman

*Please note that copies of the checklists presented in this book are available in standard or customized format directly from the authors. For more information, please contact Dr Zackrison via e-mail <zackre@hotmail.com> or postal address: R.E. Zackrison, Director, Effectiveness Consultants, Gribbylundsvägen 3, S-187 62 TÄBY, Sweden.

I

IDENTIFYING THE KIND OF HELP YOU NEED

❖

1
DO YOU REALLY NEED A CONSULTANT?

❖

WHEN DO YOU HAVE A PROBLEM?

Many managers have discarded the word '*problem*' in favour of such words and phrases as '*challenge*', '*opportunity for improvement*', '*issue*', and so on. Such managers ignore three simple facts of organizational life. First, the existence of problems is both natural and inevitable within organizations. Second, problems are not 'challenges'; it is the solving of problems that is the challenge. Third, a problem is not an 'opportunity for improvement' until it is treated as such by a competent problem-solver. Throughout this book we utilize the word 'problem' to refer to any situation that can and should be improved. If you feel uncomfortable with the word 'problem', feel free to continue fooling yourself by substituting whatever word or phrase you prefer.

One of the best definitions we have seen of 'a problem' is that it is 'the difference between what you want and what you have'. That is, a problem is the gap between intended and actual performance. As a senior manager or manager you have a problem when (1) the *current outputs* of your organization are falling short of predefined goals, expectations or standards or (2) it is likely that the *future outputs* of your organization will fall short of predefined goals, expectations or standards. There are two aspects of the preceding criteria that must be examined closely: (1) the focus on outputs as opposed to either inputs or processes and (2) the focus on both the current and the future state of your organization.

A FOCUS ON OUTPUTS

Our criteria for determining if you have a problem focus exclusively on the outputs of your organization. To understand what we mean by 'outputs' you must first understand that we view organizations as 'systems'. A simple systems view of

3

an organization (see Figure 1.1) implies that it gets inputs from its environment in the form of raw materials, people, funds, equipment, and so on. These inputs are altered by the organization through a variety of planned or unplanned transformation processes. The transformed inputs are then returned to the environment in the form of outputs, including products, profit, wastes, and so on.

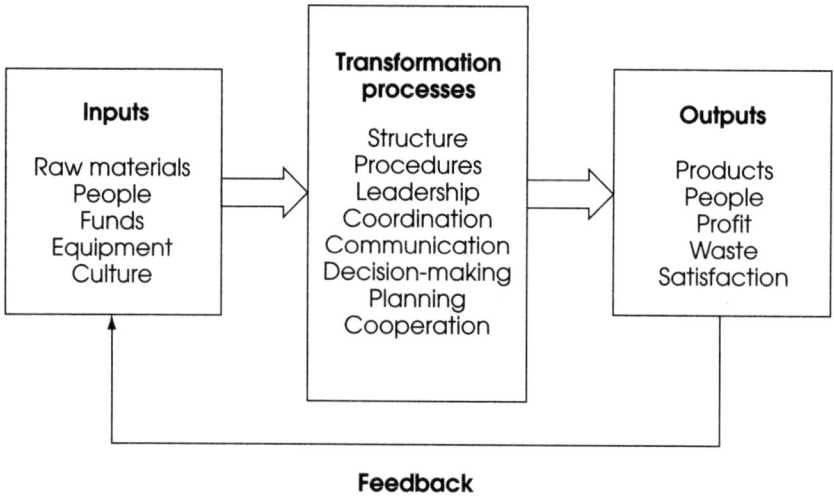

Inputs	Transformation processes	Outputs
Raw materials	Structure	Products
People	Procedures	People
Funds	Leadership	Profit
Equipment	Coordination	Waste
Culture	Communication	Satisfaction
	Decision-making	
	Planning	
	Cooperation	

Feedback

FIGURE 1.1   An open-systems view of organizations

Most senior managers readily recognize the inputs–transformation–outputs flow of the systems approach when it is applied to the conversion of raw materials (inputs) to products and wastes (outputs). As a result, they are usually reasonably adept at formulating and communicating goals for productivity, efficiency and quality, and for evaluating the degree to which outputs meet those goals. They are also aware that an organization's transformation processes do not only alter raw materials inputted into the system; they also alter human beings. People enter the organization as healthy, young, eager individuals and are returned to the environment in altered form. Some organizations return them better than they were when 'inputted' (better educated, richer, healthier), and others return them worse (injured, unhealthy, poorer).

By focusing your organization's problem-solving resources and energy on unsatisfactory organizational outputs, you avoid the trap of initiating a 'nice to do' change effort that will have little or no real positive impact upon your organization's effectiveness.

Case in point

Recently one of the authors was invited to a meeting with the Managing Director of a large manufacturing firm. Early in the meeting the MD stated that he wanted help to 'change the organization's culture'. The consultant's question, 'Why?' was met with a lot of vagueness including, 'Well, you know, we really need a better culture'. A few probing questions revealed that the organization's outputs were currently exceeding all goals for quality, productivity and profit. Employee satisfaction was high and turnover in the organization was far lower than industry averages. Equally important, there was no reason to expect anything other than continued success. Only when the mystified consultant said, 'I'm sorry, but I still don't understand what you want to accomplish' did the MD finally admit his real interest in a cultural change: 'Look, I'm a member of an executive breakfast club and almost all of my associates have initiated major cultural change efforts this year. I don't want to be seen by my peers as out of date.'

The consultant explained to the MD that an organization-wide cultural change effort is usually a very long and expensive process and that, in his case, it was unlikely to produce any significant improvements in primary organizational outputs. In fact, such a change effort would probably have a significant negative impact on his organization's productivity and profit in the short run.

The preceding case illustrates what we call a 'flavour of the month' approach to initiating organization change efforts. Instead of initiating change efforts to resolve specific output problems, many managers initiate interventions because 'everyone else is doing it'. We have found the perfect thermometer for identifying the topic that is 'hottest' today. Simply examine the titles of the books in the business section of any major airport's bookstores. You will quickly discover that at any given point in time between 30 per cent and 40 per cent of the books have the same buzz word in their title. Most of these books go to great lengths to create the impression that they have a new twist on the hot topic. For example, you will see such indispensable titles as 'The One Minute Secretary', 'Reengineering Away Stress', 'The Thai Chow Mein of Management', 'Upward Empowerment', and so on. While such 'In search of...' books often provide interesting reading, and courses, seminars and workshops based on such topics are usually very entertaining, they are usually of little or no value in helping you to improve or increase your organization's outputs.

CURRENT AND FUTURE ORIENTATION

Even though things are going well today, you may still have a problem. Our criteria infer that senior managers are responsible for both current and future organizational performance. While this may seem obvious, reality indicates that senior managers tend to spend far too much of their time grappling with current operational problems and far too little time thinking proactively and strategically about future or emerging problems. This often occurs because, in many organizations, 'fire fighting' is more visible and glamorous than fire prevention. Managers in such organizations are more likely to be recognized and rewarded for the expedient resolution of critical current problems than for anticipating, identifying and resolving less visible emergent ones. In addition, fire fighters are usually allowed to take short cuts through corporate red tape in the name of 'crisis conditions'.

While it may take bravery to fight fires, it takes alertness, persistence, attention to detail and even more bravery to prevent them, especially if management is the arsonist!

Case in point

During a six month period the number of fires in a small European town was several times higher than that of any other town of comparable size. The town council was puzzled until they realized that the increase in fires had begun at about the same time that the council had begun considering eliminating the local volunteer fire brigade in favour of contracting for the services of the more modern full-time fire department from a neighbouring city. An investigation discovered that a couple of the volunteer firemen were starting the fires in order to prove that the volunteer fire brigade was still needed.

Although the above case may appear to be an extreme example, it is far more typical than you might assume. How many fires are started in your organization by people trying to demonstrate that their positions are essential?

Combining the preceding two cases, your organization has a problem if – and only if – your outputs are currently falling short of agreed goals and expectations or they are likely to do so at some defined point in the future. If outputs are satisfactory and are likely to continue to be so, you don't have a problem!

RECOGNIZING PROBLEMS WHEN YOU HAVE THEM

How do you know when you have a problem? Most of us know instinctively when we have a problem in our organizations, that is, when there is, or is likely to be, a gap between expected and actual performance. We may not have a clear picture of what is wrong or how things ought to be or could be, but we somehow sense that the situation should not be as it is. Therefore, instead of asking: 'How do I know if I have a problem in my organization?', it may be more appropriate to ask: 'When should I start committing resources to things that I feel may be a problem?'

Case in point

Many years ago one of the authors taught an MBA level course in advanced decision-making tools and methods. During the eleven weeks of the course participants were presented with numerous complex, statistically based tools and techniques intended to produce the most rational, objective decisions possible in a variety of situations. On the last day of the course the author informed his MBA candidates that the 'litmus test for the effectiveness of any decision-making method presented during the course is to take a minute and reflect on how it "feels" once it is made. If it feels "wrong", then it is likely that there is something that you have missed.'

Our recommendation to you is that, no matter what the rational, objective data says, if you don't 'feel right' about a given condition within your organization, then there is a good chance that it is not right. This is not some mystical occurrence; it is simply the result of the fact that we record a lot of valuable data into our subconscious as we go through our day-to-day lives. This data may be stored in remote nooks and crannies of our brains, but it is nonetheless valid.

One of senior management's responsibilities is to ensure that they are getting all of the information needed to sense emerging problems before they become serious. Many senior managers are not fully aware of existing or emerging problems in their organization because someone at a level below them is making sure that problems are not brought to their attention. In many organizations middle and even senior managers fear that admitting to problems in their area of responsibility will be interpreted as a sign of their own weakness as managers. As a result, they hide their 'weaknesses' from their superiors and, perhaps, even from themselves.

In some cases, concealing problems is an intentional strategy of deceit.

Case in point

For three years in a row the regional plant manager of a large national manufacturing company had received considerable recognition and monetary rewards because his plant had consistently exceeded production quotas. When the plant manager resigned to accept a more lucrative position in a competing firm his former management was quite upset. Within three months their frustration turned to anger when they discovered that monthly reports from their former plant manager had portrayed only the positive side of what had been happening at his plant. For example, he had conveniently forgotten to mention that he had been postponing preventive maintenance in order to push production levels as high as possible in the short run. As a result, plant production equipment was in critical need of costly, time consuming repairs that would require that it be shut down during the company's peak production period.

In many organizations senior executives are shielded from unpleasant realities by well meaning (and, occasionally, not so well meaning) subordinates. Irving Janis, of *groupthink* fame, called such people 'mind-guards'. Mind-guards ensure that their superiors only hear modified and more palatable versions of the truth. Many executives encourage such filtering behaviour by communicating, in words or actions, 'don't bring me bad news'.

WHEN SHOULD YOU ATTEND TO A PROBLEM?

Although you are probably familiar with the old adage: *'The squeaky wheel gets the most grease!'*, you may be less familiar with its two corollaries:

1.   *If two wheels are already squeaking, it is harder to notice when a third begins to squeak,* and
2.   *Squeaky wheels do not get greased until they are squeaking so loudly that they disturb the driver.*

In too many organizations, 'squeaks' are ignored until they reach a critical decibel level. Even then, the causes of the squeak may receive little attention because other factors (louder squeaks) are absorbing all available problem-solving resources and energy.

Just because a wheel is squeaking does not mean that it should be attended to. Not all problems are worthy of your own or your organization's attention. The following criteria are designed to help you decide when you should attend to a problem - and when you should simply let it go.

A problem should be attended to if:

O   it is something that has a significant negative implication for current or future organizational outputs, such as costs, productivity, quality, employee turnover, customer service, and so on;

○   it is something about which you and/or other key members of your organ-
    ization feel significantly dissatisfied, disappointed, and/or frustrated;

○   it is something over which you have some control or, at least, something
    that is within your sphere of influence; and

○   in order to improve this particular situation you and other significant
    members of your organization are willing to sacrifice the opportunity to
    do something else.

DO YOU REALLY NEED AN EXTERNAL CONSULTANT?

Not all problems within an organization require the assistance of an external consultant. In fact, one of the quickest ways to demotivate otherwise dedicated,
creative internal staff is to bring in an external consultant who is paid a lot of
money to tell you the same things that your internal staff have been trying to tell
you for several years. An external consultant is only needed when (1) your organization lacks the problem-solving resources necessary to deal effectively with the
problem *and* (2) leaving the problem unresolved will cost more than it will cost to
bring in an external consultant. If either of these conditions is not met then an
external consultant is *not* the answer!

An external consultant may also be necessary if (1) the problem is so technical
that there is no justifiable reason to invest time and money to develop your
internal competence, (2) the problem is non-recurring and there is no ongoing
need for the skills that the consultant will use to solve the problem, or (3) someone is needed to temporarily fill a competency gap until members of your organization can gain the skills or find time to deal with the problem.

COMBINING INTERNAL AND EXTERNAL PROBLEM-SOLVING RESOURCES

In many problem-solving situations the wisest and most economical strategy is to
combine internal and external problem-solving resources. Combining internal and
external resources has many benefits, including:

○   enhancing the skills, competence and self-respect of internal staff mem-
    bers;

○   development of an internal resource that can be used to deal with future
    situations;

○   significantly reducing the costs of solving the problem;

○   avoiding the resistance that internal staff often demonstrate towards pro-
    grammes coming from the 'outside';

○   development of programmes and solutions that are better tailored to your
    organization's unique culture, traditions, and so on;

○   The more internal resources you use and develop, the less reliant your organization will be on external support.

SUMMARY

As we have pointed out in this chapter, the first prerequisite for calling in a consultant is that you already have – or can reasonably anticipate – a 'problem'. As a senior manager your organization has a problem if – and only if – your outputs are currently falling short of agreed goals and expectations or they are likely to do so at some defined point in the future. If outputs are satisfactory and are likely to continue to be so, you don't have a problem!

But simply having a 'problem' is not sufficient reason for investing your scarce human and financial resources in external assistance. You must first determine if the problem is worth attending to and, if so, if it is best resolved by your own internal staff, by external consulting help – or by a combination of the two. If you have determined that you require the assistance of an external consultant, the next chapter will help you to determine which type of consultant is likely to be of most value.

2

WHAT TYPE OF CONSULTANT DO YOU NEED?

❖

Once you recognize that you have a serious problem in your organization and that you need some form of external assistance to resolve it, you are about to enter what we call the 'consultant jungle'. The first step in finding your way in the consultant jungle is to recognize that not every individual who calls him/herself a 'consultant' is, in fact, qualified to work as a consultant. In this chapter we examine five broad categories of people who frequently offer their services as 'consultants': Academics, Helping Hands, Training Specialists, Expert Consultants, and Process Consultants.

We have chosen these five categories for two reasons. First, the majority of the individuals or firms that call themselves consultants fall into one of these five categories. Thus, in discussing them we will cover most of the individuals or firms populating the consultant jungle. Second, the five categories provide an excellent framework for distinguishing between 'true' and 'false' consultants, that is, between those who *are consultants* and those who *merely claim to be consultants*. Our frame of reference for making this distinction is found in the title of a song from the 1940s – '*It ain't what'cha do, it's the way that'cha do it!*' As this chapter will clearly demonstrate, it is not what people do that qualifies them as 'consultants'; it is the way that they do whatever it is that they do.

ACADEMICS

We begin with Academics because they provide an excellent example of people who often market themselves as consultants but seldom perform as such. In addition, more and more Academics seem to be calling themselves consultants, especially those in the management sciences. The problem is that Academics and business executives/managers live in two very different worlds in which success is based on widely differing goals, actions and values.

Case in point

With only his dissertation remaining for his doctorate, one of the authors left the university and returned to the business community. Once there he quickly discovered that the pressures of his management position made completing his dissertation impossible. As a result he returned to academia as a Research Assistant for two terms in order to have the time and support he required to complete his dissertation.

On the first day of his assistantship the supervising professor of his department assigned him a research project which appeared to be fairly simple and straightforward. The author threw himself energetically into the project and, after a week, proudly presented his results to his supervising professor. 'Oh', said the very surprised professor. 'Are you done already? Are you quite sure that you have considered all possible variables?' 'I think so', said the author, 'but if you find any omissions I would be pleased to consider them.' A week later the professor informed the author that his work on the original project was 'acceptable' and he was given a new research project, along with the warning to be 'a bit more thorough this time'. When the author submitted the results for the second project three weeks later the professor accepted them with considerable reluctance. He returned to the author the next day and said, 'Didn't I tell you to be more thorough on this project?' 'Yes', replied the author, 'and I thought I was. Can you tell me what is wrong with my results?' 'You developed them too quickly', said the professor. 'We had expected this project to take several weeks.'

Needless to say, the author learned. The next project he was given could have easily been completed 'thoroughly' in three to four weeks. The author took a total of fifteen weeks before submitting his results, even though he had actually completed the project two months earlier. After reviewing the results the professor said, 'Now that is much better; you finally understood the benefits of being thorough!'

In an article entitled 'The Academic Consultant', Furnham and Pendleton (1991) present an interesting comparison of academics and consultants. We present this comparison, in slightly modified form, in Table 2.1. While the picture of Academics portrayed in the table is clearly biased, we feel it is more true than false in far too many cases.

TABLE 2.1 A comparison of Academics and consultants

	Academics	Consultants
Major aims	Insight and knowledge	Change
Time scale	Low urgency	High urgency
Type of solution sought	Academically sound	Realistically practical
Source of insight	Research	Experience
Level of complexity	High	Low
Cost-benefit analysis	Irrelevant	Crucial
Means of persuasion	Theory backed by data	Data backed by argument
Preferred medium of presentation	Written	Face-to-face
Reaction to resistance	Defensiveness	Management
Dealing with uncertainty	Statistically	Realistically
Dealing with conflict	Avoidance	Confrontation

Source: Adapted from Adrian Furnham and David Pendleton (1991), 'The Academic Consultant', *Journal of General Management,* 17, pp. 13–19.

Many of the differences between Academics and consultants may be due to the fact that Academics tend to begin with a puzzle: 'How are these parts related?' Consultants, on the other hand, usually start with a problem: 'How can we solve this?' (As a former Academic, Dr Zackrison is fond of saying, 'When I was an Academic I was fascinated by theories; now I'm fascinated with making them work!')

Another key distinction between Academics and consultants is found in the question, 'Who needs whom?' Typically, Academics need you – that is, they are dependent on the support of the business community for the funds, research venues/situations and the support required to conduct their academic studies. A good consultant, on the other hand, does not need you; you need him/her, otherwise you would not have invited them in.

Because Academics and consultants differ significantly in so many ways, they typically approach the process of 'consulting' in quite different ways; and the differences in their approaches are bound to produce significantly different results. For example, because the primary aim of Academics is to achieve insight, understanding or knowledge, they are often satisfied when they have gained a better understanding of the issue under investigation. While effective consultants also adhere to sound research techniques, they are typically more action-orientated and are not satisfied until they have developed concrete solutions to the problem(s) at hand.

It should be clear from the above that we do not consider Academics to be consultants. In our opinion, Academics only become consultants when they cease thinking/acting like Academics and begin thinking/acting like consultants. That does not mean that Academics cannot function effectively as consultants. They can be exceptionally talented consultants if they are able to incorporate the strengths of their academic backgrounds into the more practical world of business. However, because Academic and consulting roles are basically incompatible, an individual must be clear when s/he is wearing an Academic hat and when s/he is wearing a consultant hat – and *never* try to put on both hats at the same time.

Case in point

One of our colleagues is a highly competent Academic *and* a very skilled consultant. In his Academic role he conducted a comprehensive study of effective and ineffective leadership behaviour in large organizations. As part of that study he carefully observed the supervisory, management and executive staff within one organization for a period of several months. Although his observations clearly revealed several leadership problems within that organization, he did nothing to help the organization to resolve those problems. Instead, he used them as a source of knowledge about leadership problems and the impact of such problems on the effectiveness of the organization. After completion of his research project, he exchanged his 'Academic hat' for a 'consultant hat' and returned to the organization where he worked for several weeks helping management to resolve some of the leadership issues that he had identified while conducting his research. In short, he functioned as both an Academic and a consultant within this organization, but not at the same time.

We (as former Academics) vigorously applaud business community support for academic research, especially in the areas of organizational management, behaviour and dynamics. The results of such research are invaluable to us as consultants – and to our clients. However, you must not confuse academic research with consulting efforts intended to resolve significant current or emerging problems within your organization. In fact, when you and your management team are struggling frantically with a major emerging problem, the last thing you need is an Academic running around doing research. Paradoxically, if qualified Academics are not allowed to conduct research within organizations experiencing significant problems, our future understanding of the causes and effects of those problems is likely to be significantly reduced.

HELPING HANDS

Although some Helping Hands like to call themselves consultants and even management consultants, it is far more appropriate and less confusing to refer to them as 'temporary employees'. Helping Hands are individuals brought into your organization on a strictly temporary basis to perform tasks normally performed by your regular employees. For example, they might be engaged to fill a temporary void caused by the extended illness of a key employee or to catch up on a back-log of work caused by a temporary surge in the demand for your organization's products and/or services. Helping Hands are expected to fit themselves into your workforce and function as full-time or part-time temporary 'producers', contributing in the same way as permanent, full-time or part-time employees in similar roles. They are supervised as any other member of your regular staff would be in the same position and their performance is evaluated in the same ways as that of regular permanent employees.

Helping Hands may be paired with your existing personnel to serve as 'models' to demonstrate the ways in which specific tasks should be performed. In this instance, their usefulness ends when existing staff have acquired sufficient understanding, skill and judgement to perform in their roles as proficiently as the Helping Hands.

TRAINING SPECIALISTS

There are two types of individuals who offer their services as Training Specialists – Training Providers and Training Consultants.

Training Providers are individuals or firms that market pre-packaged, off-the-shelf training programmes. When one of our clients tells us that they are considering the purchase of such a programme we usually respond by waving red caution flags as vigorously as possible. Far too many of those who market pre-packaged, off-the-shelf training programmes can best be described as hammer-salesmen who treat all problems they encounter as if they were nails! In addition to (or because of) their questionable relevance to organizational needs, pre-packaged, off-the-shelf training programmes frequently yield results that fall far short of expectations and which are difficult to sustain.

However, not all off-the-shelf training programmes are of little or no value. Clearly, such programmes can be beneficial when:

O   the concepts presented by the course are generic in nature, that is, they are of equal value to participants, regardless of their organization. Such training might include basic communications skills, presentation skills and negotiation skills.

O   the concepts are best taught to groups of individuals who do not work together on a day-to-day basis. For example, courses in self-awareness or group dynamics are often far more beneficial when participants feel free to take risks and to experiment with different behaviours. This usually works best when the training group is composed of relative strangers.

O   participants can significantly benefit from the insights of people from different organizations, functions, levels, and so on. For example, participants in our Consultant Training Programme benefit greatly from the fact that they come from a wide variety of cultures, organizations and professional backgrounds.

O   the costs of producing a programme tailored specifically to your in-house needs would exceed the benefits of such a programme.

No matter how valuable the programme offered by a Training Provider might be, we still do not accept them as consultants. At best, they are marketers and sales-people.

Training Consultants are individuals or firms with the professional skills and experience necessary to:

O   assess the training needs of individuals and/or groups within your organization;

O   custom design training programmes intended to meet specific, prioritized training needs;

O   assist in the implementation of these programmes within your organization;

O   facilitate and/or, when possible and appropriate, enable your own staff to facilitate the training programmes developed; and/or

O   assist you in the evaluation of the results of implemented training activities.

A Training Consultant is likely to be your best choice if (1) the cause of the problem(s) is clearly identified as a lack of the individual knowledge or skills necessary to effectively perform current or future tasks, (2) a tailor-made training programme is clearly the best way of providing those skills, and (3) no one in your organization is capable of designing and implementing the training necessary.

We classify Training Consultants as 'true' consultants *if* they perform their tasks in accordance with the following criteria:

O   In the process of assessing training needs, they actively explore the possibility that the problem(s) under investigation may require a non-training solution. For example, if they have been called in to assess training needs in the area of communications, they are open to the possibility that poor communication might be the result of ineffective organizational structures, inappropriate power games, and so on, not a lack of communications skills.

O   They are proactive in their approach to training needs, that is, instead of waiting for someone to say, 'We need a course in...', they scan your organization to identify and help you to provide for emerging training needs.

O   They are aware of and constantly emphasize the benefits of providing training to intact work groups using real-life, relevant content and concepts.

O   They constantly seek ways to ensure the internalization and sustainability of the training that they provide, including insisting that participants are supported, recognized and rewarded for application of newly learned skills and concepts.

EXPERT CONSULTANTS

Expert Consultants typically possess in-depth knowledge, skill and experience in a relatively narrow, specialized, and often technical area. Their services are most appropriate when you need to solve a one-time-only, non-recurring technical or highly specialized problem. The primary role of Expert Consultants is to use their professional skills and methods to analyse your problem situation and recommend solutions. In most cases, their assignment will end once they submit their conclusions and recommendations. However, they may also assist in the implementation of their recommendations.

One of the major risks of using Expert Consultants is that their recommendations often fail because they lack the committed support of the members of the client organization or because employees feel that the Expert Consultant's solutions were imposed on them in an arbitrary, uncaring and/or insensitive manner. Problems may also arise if the Expert Consultant is perceived as having more influence than your permanent employees because s/he is a 'consultant', not because s/he has more knowledge or skill or because s/he can develop better solutions. It is not difficult to imagine the consequences if you accept recommendations from an external Expert Consultant that are identical (or even similar) to recommendations that many of your organization's members have been trying to get you to 'hear' for years.

PROCESS CONSULTANTS

The biggest difference between Expert Consultants and Process Consultants is that Process Consultants seldom recommend solutions. Instead, they prefer to work collaboratively with the organization's leaders and members, helping them to identify, clarify, prioritize and resolve problems within their own organization. As a result, the services of a Process Consultant are most appropriate when the success of the consulting effort is dependent upon building commitment from key organization members to the solutions to be implemented.

One of the stated goals of most Process Consultants is to transfer their skills and knowledge to the members of your organization, thus increasing the ability of your existing personnel to deal with similar problems in the future, without the assistance of an external consultant. Typical assignments for Process Consultants include helping you and your senior managers to:

O   develop and implement a change in your organization's culture, such as moving from an autocratic to a more participative management style;

O   reformulate your organization's core mission and bring all departments and functions of your organization into line with that mission;

O   design and implement a more appropriate organizational structure;

O   develop a strategy for more effective utilization of your organization's scarce resources;

O   improve the level of cooperation (or reduce the level of conflicts) between functional and structural units within your organization; and/or

O   develop and gain commitment to a comprehensive strategic plan for your organization and its primary functions/components.

The past experiences of members of your organization with people who called themselves consultants may have an adverse effect on the success of consulting effort conducted by a Process Consultant. Specifically, if you or your organization's managers are used to working with Expert Consultants, they may view a Process Consultant's attempts to collaborate with them as a lack of competence, avoidance of responsibility or as a lack of self-confidence. If members of your organization have felt resentment towards Helping Hands who did the same job as they do, at what they perceive as several times the pay, they may consciously or unconsciously resist cooperating with the Process Consultant.

CONSULTANT TYPES AND THE PURPOSES OF THE CONSULTATION

When properly matched with the assignment, each of the five types of 'consultants' described in this chapter can provide a beneficial service to your organization. In order to create such a match, you and your management team must agree the specific results that you expect from your consultant and be aware of the degree to which each of the consultant types is likely to meet those expectations. There are seven legitimate purposes that might be served by a consultant. These can be arranged into the hierarchy presented in Figure 2.1. Table 2.2 summarizes the degree to which you can expect each of the five consulting types to provide you with each of the seven levels of services defined by the hierarchy.

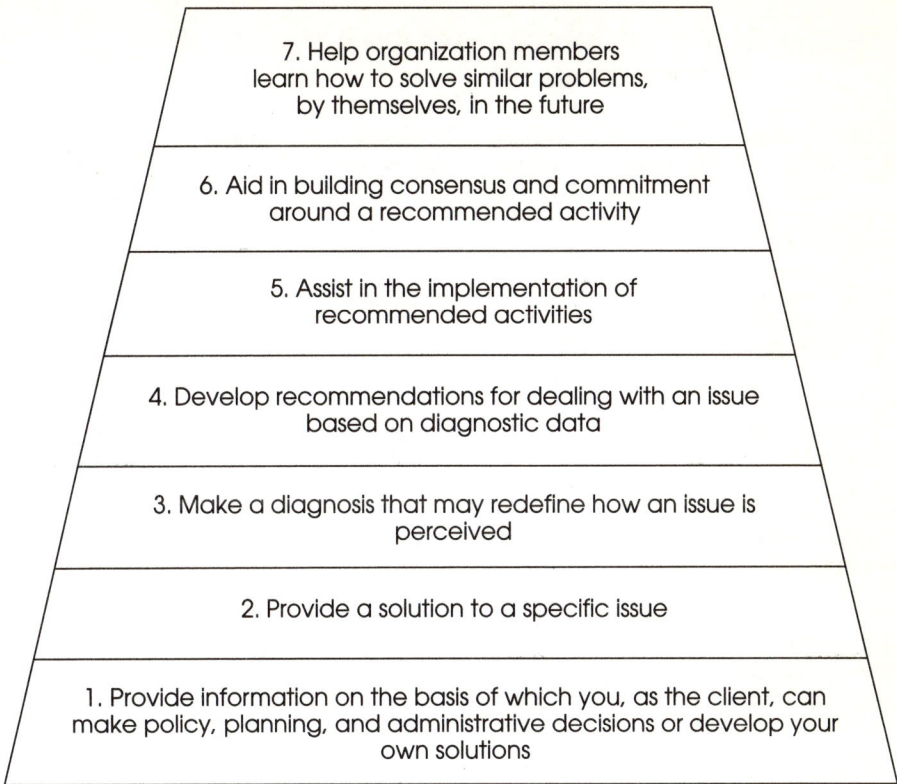

7. Help organization members learn how to solve similar problems, by themselves, in the future

6. Aid in building consensus and commitment around a recommended activity

5. Assist in the implementation of recommended activities

4. Develop recommendations for dealing with an issue based on diagnostic data

3. Make a diagnosis that may redefine how an issue is perceived

2. Provide a solution to a specific issue

1. Provide information on the basis of which you, as the client, can make policy, planning, and administrative decisions or develop your own solutions

FIGURE 2.1   A hierarchy of consulting purposes

Source: Adapted from Arthur N. Turner (1982), 'Consulting is More than Giving Advice', *Harvard Business Review*, September–October, pp. 120–9.

As Table 2.2 indicates, Academics cannot be expected to provide services at any level of the hierarchy, at least not intentionally. The reason for this is simple. Academic research is primarily for the benefit of the researcher and his/her sponsoring institution and seldom has any direct benefit to the client serving as the subject of the research.

Because Helping Hands are brought into the organization to do a specific job, they should not be expected to fulfil any of the seven levels on the hierarchy unless, of course, it is a requirement of the position that they are temporarily filling. For example, they may make recommendations if they are filling a temporary post that normally makes recommendations in the problem area being addressed.

Training Consultants and, to some degree, Training Providers, may be expected

TABLE 2.2 Primary purposes of the five types of consultants

Hierarchical levels	Academics	Helping Hands	Training Specialists	Expert Consultants	Process Consultants
7. Help members learn how to solve similar problems, by themselves, in the future	No	No	When acting consultatively	Seldom	Consultants' primary responsibility
6. Aid in building consensus and commitment	No	No	When acting consultatively	Seldom	Consultants' primary responsibility
5. Assist in the implementation	No	As part of assigned task	Conduct training programmes	Seldom	Facilitate implementations in collaboration with internal staff
4. Recommend measures for dealing with an issue/problem	No	Seldom	Recommend training based on needs assessment	Consultants' primary responsibility	Facilitate strategy development by internal staff
3. Conduct a diagnosis that may redefine how an issue is perceived	No	Seldom	Restricted to assessment of training needs	Consultants' primary responsibility	Consultants' primary responsibility
2. Provide a solution to a specific issue	Unintentionally	As part of assigned task	Only for training programmes	Consultants' primary responsibility	Seldom
1. Provide information	Unintentionally	As part of assigned task	Seldom	Consultants' primary responsibility	Seldom

Source: Adapted from Arthur N. Turner (1982), 'Consulting is More than Giving Advice', Harvard Business Review, September–October, pp. 120–9

to provide services at each of the five lower levels of the hierarchy but their focus will normally be restricted to specifically defined training problems. In fact, Training Consultants are often in a unique position to support the development of consensus about and commitment to specific change efforts. For example, a change in an organization's leadership culture, as conducted by a Process Consultant, may require a significant amount of training in basic leadership skills. If designed and delivered properly, the training can serve as a framework for helping participants to understand, accept and commit to the changes in the overall leadership culture of their organization.

Expert Consultants function primarily at the lower four levels of the hierarchy. Their forte is analysing and providing solutions to problems within their specific functional or technical areas. Many Expert Consultants consider their task to be complete when they have submitted their recommendation. The most frequent exception to this is when the nature of the Expert Consultant's solutions is so technical or specialized, that it requires their continued assistance during the implementation phase. For example, an organization may engage an Expert Consultant to design *and* install a turnkey computer networking system. In such a situation, the consultant's assignment may even include training the organization's personnel in the use of that system. Here the Expert Consultant is not 'involved in the implementation'. Rather, s/he is the primary implementor. It is important to note that Expert Consultants seldom involve themselves in helping client organizations to be less reliant on consulting help in the future. In fact, there is considerable evidence to indicate that many Expert Consultants actively seek out and exploit ways to make their clients increasingly dependent on them and their firms.

Process Consultants typically provide services at levels 3–7 of the hierarchy. In fact, most Process Consultants will insist on conducting a diagnosis of the situation (level 3) before moving upward in the hierarchy. No matter which level they are working at, Process Consultants will usually be involved only to the degree that your internal resources lack the skills necessary to do the work required. This is based on their conviction that, to do otherwise, would deny the members of your organization an opportunity to learn to rely upon themselves and could induce unnecessary dependency on the consultant. Process Consultants typically excel at levels 6 and 7 of the hierarchy and are likely to employ a variety of techniques to induce high levels of internal commitment in your change process, building support for actions necessary for its success.

The lower five levels of the hierarchy represent the 'traditional' purposes of most consulting efforts, that is, it is at these levels that consultants have traditionally focused most of their time and energy. And it is at these levels that most clients expect consultants to perform. Recently, however, both clients and consultants have become increasingly aware of the importance of levels 6 and 7 and are beginning to accept them as legitimate and essential purposes for consultants rather than as unnecessary 'fluff' as many critics believed them to be in the past.

We have found the hierarchy of consulting purposes to be invaluable in discussions with potential clients. It helps us and our clients to clarify and agree on desired outcomes, negotiate the scope of a prospective consultation, and make informed decisions about the contents of consulting agreements. Many potential client–consultant conflicts can be avoided if you ensure early on that your expectations for the project are at the same level as those of the consultant that you engage.

Case in point

A recent graduate of our Consultant Training Programme was having difficulties with the Managing Director of a client organization and asked for our help. True to her training as a Process Consultant our graduate had collected considerable data about the strengths and weaknesses of her client organization. Much of the data indicated that the MD and his executives were one of the major causes of many of the problems within the organization. The executives were perceived as pulling in different directions, failing to implement agreed decisions, and too focused on operative issues as opposed to strategic ones. The MD was seen as 'too weak' to adequately manage his executives. In addition, there was a common perception that the organization's structure was too complex, too top heavy, and contained too many levels.

The consultant suggested that the MD gather his team for a four-day session during which she, the consultant, would present the results of the assessment and work with the executive committee. The specific goals of the workshop would be 'to identify and develop solutions to prioritized problems within the organization'. Her suggestion was met with anger from the MD: 'I did not hire you to tie up my entire executive committee for four days! I hired you to tell me what is wrong with my organization and tell me how to fix it. I expect a full report, including appropriate recommendations, on my desk within three days.'

What happened? The consultant had assumed that she was engaged to produce results at levels 5 and 6 of the hierarchy. The client thought that he had engaged an Expert Consultant who would produce level 4 results. Who was in the wrong? Both the consultant and the MD made a serious error in not clarifying and agreeing on the type of consultant or the level of results to be produced by the consulting effort.

THE APPROACH OF THE THREE 'TRUE' CONSULTANTS

Although Training Consultants, Expert Consultants and Process Consultants may work at the same level of the preceding hierarchy, they are likely to differ substantially in their approach to the tasks inherent in that level. For example, if a

Training Consultant is given the task of 'improving delegation' in an organization, s/he will typically begin by conducting an assessment of potential participants' current level of knowledge and competence in the area of delegation.

Expert Consultants will tend to limit the scope of their diagnosis to their specific area of expertise. If tasked to 'improve delegation', they will typically conduct an analysis of how delegation is currently being done in the organization, compare it with their own model of how delegation should be done, and then make recommendations for bringing the organization in line with their model.

Process Consultants typically prefer to conduct broader diagnoses to ensure that they identify the root causes of the problem being investigated. In addition, they usually prefer to more actively involve organizational members than do either the Training Consultant or Expert Consultant. As a result, if asked to 'improve delegation' they will typically conduct individual and group interviews with key members of the organization. In conducting these interviews they are likely to probe into such peripheral areas as decision-making, empowerment, motivation, communication, and so on.

There are crucial differences between the Training Consultant, Expert Consultant and Process Consultant that you should consider. Of the three, the Training Consultant is usually most aware of what is required to change individual attitudes and behaviour. The Expert Consultant is typically most aware of what is required to change the technical aspects of the system in which s/he specializes. The Process Consultant is typically most aware of how any given change effort is likely to affect group and organizational dynamics.

CHAPTER SUMMARY

One of the primary distinctions between the five types of 'consultants' presented in this chapter is the focus of their activities and interventions. Table 2.3 provides you with an easy reference for identifying what you can expect each of the five consulting types to do for you and your organization.

TABLE 2.3   The primary functions of the five types of consultants

	Primary focus of consulting activities	When should you consider engaging this type of consultant?
Academics	Conducting academic research intended to broaden the understanding of a specific function or process within organizations	Academic research should be actively supported when – and only when – said support will not interfere with the organization's ability to deal effectively with current or emerging problems
Helping Hands	Performing tasks inherent in the temporary position that they have been engaged to fill	When you have a short-term need for a competency that is normally available among your full-time staff
Training Specialist	Improving the skills and/or changing the attitudes of specific individuals/groups within the organization	When you need to provide specific employees or groups of employees with specific skills or knowledge or to change the attitudes of those to be trained
Expert Consultants	Providing expert solutions to specific technical problems	When you have a short-term, non-recurrent need for specific technical skills or knowledge that is not readily available internally
Process Consultants	Improving the overall effectiveness of the organization and/or of a specific function or group within the organization	When you need to resolve a problem while simultaneously developing the ability of internal staff members to effectively deal with similar problems in the future

PART I
CHECKLISTS

❖

AN INTRODUCTION TO THE CHECKLISTS*

Following each of the four parts of this book we provide a series of 'checklists' designed to help you to apply the content of the preceding chapters. The questions in most of the checklists are not easy to answer because they require 'knowing what you don't know'. To avoid the risks inherent in this Catch 22 situation, we recommend that you use the checklists as the basis for in-depth discussions between yourself and other key members of your organization. In fact, you may even invite consultant candidates to participate in some of your discussions.

To maximize the value of your discussions, we suggest that you and others with whom you intend to discuss the checklists begin by responding individually to each checklist. Whenever possible, try to respond as quickly and spontaneously as possible based on what you feel, not what you think. Then take some time to ponder your initial responses in more depth. Once everyone has had time to respond individually to the checklists, gather them together and go through each item in detail. As you do so, avoid the trap of assuming that similar ratings mean agreement. For example, everyone may have come to the conclusion that you need an external consultant – but the reasons for this conclusion may differ greatly – and it is the reasons that you need to understand and agree upon!

We also recommend that you don't rush any of the checklists that you think may be of value. Making the right decisions about engaging, managing and evaluating consultants requires considerable time and rushed decisions can be quite costly.

*For details of how to obtain further copies of the checklists please see page xi.

DO YOU NEED EXTERNAL HELP

The following series of six checklists have been designed to help you determine whether you have a problem that requires external consulting assistance. It is important that you complete the checklists in order. If you are dissatisfied with your answers to any of the checklists, move on to the next checklist:

Checklist I.1
Are you prepared to identify problems should they arise?

The questions in this checklist focus on the degree to which you are aware of problems within your organization and your degree of responsiveness once a problem has been identified.

Yes ? No   1. Things are going well in our organization today.

Yes ? No   2. People at all levels of our organization keep their managers well informed of existing and emerging problems.

Yes ? No   3. People at all levels of our organization feel comfortable admitting their mistakes and reporting both current and emerging problems.

Yes ? No   4. People at all levels of our organization can be trusted to be open and honest about any problems that they are experiencing.

Yes ? No   5. When problems occur in our organization the first reaction, especially at the senior level, is to fix the problem. Once the problem is fixed we work together to minimize chances of its recurrence.

Yes ? No   6. When problems occur in our organization, especially at the senior level, we consciously avoid such destructive tactics as finger pointing, scapegoating, defensiveness, and so on.

Yes ? No   7. People at all levels of our organization actively seek out and quickly respond at the first sign of problems

Yes ? No   8. People at all levels of our organization openly share their perceptions of problems across functional, departmental and hierarchical boundaries.

If you have answered 'No' or '?' to any of the above questions, it may be wise to spend some time working on your organization's climate. You should be especially concerned if your answers indicate weaknesses in how your senior executives and managers deal with the identification, communication and resolution of problems within your organization.

Alternatively, you may benefit by contracting with a consultant to conduct a thorough assessment of your organization's current and potential strengths and weaknesses. The rationale behind this suggestion is the same as the rationale for annual physical examinations by a qualified doctor; they are trained to see things that we may miss!

Checklist I.2
Do you have a problem now?

In Chapter 1 we defined a problem as a current or potential gap between actual and expected outputs. Outputs can be defined in financial terms such as profit and return on investment; in production terms such as productivity and efficiency; in human terms such as turnover and employee satisfaction levels; in customer terms such as market share, customer satisfaction, and brand recognition; and/or in environmental terms such as community development and compliance ratings, and so on. Before answering the two questions below, we suggest that you gather your senior management team and develop a comprehensive list of the outputs that you expect from your organization. Once your list of outputs is complete, make sure that each output is stated in measurable terms. That is, don't be satisfied with statements such as 'customer satisfaction'. Instead, agree on measurable customer satisfaction targets, for example, '85 per cent of our customers will rate our service as very satisfactory at any point in time'.

Once you have your list of desired outputs, answer the following two questions for each significant output area:

Yes ? No   1. Our organization is currently meeting or exceeding our goals, expectations and standards in this output area.

Yes ? No   2. We have carefully scanned our internal and external environments and are confident that our organization will continue to meet or exceed our goals, expectations and standards in this output area in the foreseeable future.

If your answer to both questions is 'yes' and you are confident that your answers to checklist I.1 are accurate, congratulations! You and your fellow managers are either extremely lucky or extremely skilled. Either way, the last thing you need right now is a consultant. You would be wiser to use your resources to celebrate your success to ensure that it continues.

Checklist I.3
Should something be done about the problem?

You should attend to a problem if and only if you can answer 'Yes' to all four of the following questions:

Yes ? No   1. The problem has a significant negative implication for our current or future organizational outputs, for example, costs, productivity, quality, employee turnover, customer service, and so on.

Yes ? No   2. The problem is something about which a significant number of key members of our organization feel significantly dissatisfied, disappointed, and/or frustrated.

Yes ? No   3. The problem is something over which we have some control or, at least, something that is within our sphere of influence; and

Yes ? No   4. In order to improve this particular situation a significant number of key members of our organization are willing to sacrifice the opportunity to do something else.

If you have answered 'Yes' to all four of the preceding questions, the problem is yours and you should probably do something about it. A '?' in response to any question indicates the need for further investigation and clarification. A 'No' for any of the four questions indicates that you should not invest your own time or energy into trying to resolve the problem, in which case the problem should be ignored or passed on to someone else for resolution.

Checklist I.4
Do you have internal resources to solve the problem?

In many problem-solving situations, the more you utilize your organization's own internal personnel, the less reliant you and your organization will be on external support. The following checklist is designed to help you to determine the degree to which your organization already has the internal resources required to deal with this specific problem situation.

Yes ? No 1. There are people in our organization with the skills neces-
                sary to gather and organize all data necessary to fully under-
                stand our situation.

Yes ? No 2. There are people in our organization with the skills neces-
                sary to thoroughly analyse the above data, including the
                abilities to distinguish between the symptoms of our prob-
                lem and its root causes.

Yes ? No 3. There are people in our organization with the skills neces-
                sary to identify obstacles, both personal and organizational,
                which are likely to interfere with our efforts to effectively
                resolve our problem situation.

Yes ? No 4. There are people in our organization with the skills neces-
                sary to develop realistic and effective solutions to our prob-
                lem situation.

Yes ? No 5. There are people in our organization with the skills neces-
                sary to develop an effective strategy for implementing the
                chosen solution to our problem situation (that is, to develop
                an 'action plan').

Yes ? No 6. There are people in our organization with the skills neces-
                sary to implement the selected solutions, including the abili-
                ties (a) to manage the change process, (b) to coordinate and
                integrate the efforts of all people involved, (c) to monitor
                reactions and responses from significant individuals and
                groups who are likely to be impacted, and (d) to identify the
                need for and make necessary adjustments to the action plan.

Yes ? No 7. The people in our organization with the skills necessary to
                assist in developing and implementing solutions to this
                problem can be relatively easily accessed and mobilized.

The preceding questionnaire will give you an indication of the areas in which you
may be able to utilize your existing internal staff to deal with this problem situation. It will also indicate areas in which you may want to develop your internal
staff's capabilities or bring in external assistance. For example, a negative
response to question 4 indicates that your existing staff are weak in problem-
solving skills. Although you may benefit from bringing in a consultant to help you
in this area, you may benefit even more by investing in improving your internal
problem-solving capabilities.

If you have answered 'Yes' to the majority of the preceding questions, you are clearly indicating that you already have the internal resources necessary to resolve your problem situation and, in question 7, that these resources can be readily mobilized. However, as the next checklist will indicate, there may be valid reasons why it is unwise to rely too heavily on your internal resources.

Checklist I.5
Should your internal resources be utilized?

Yes ? No   1.   The internal people available for this assignment will not be unduly affected by their own biases and vested interests and will be able to act without fear of saying things which may be upsetting to their superiors, peers and others.

Yes ? No   2.   These internal people available for the above tasks have sufficient status and credibility to be accepted by our organizational executives, managers and informal organizational leaders.

Yes ? No   3.   Utilizing internal people is unlikely to interfere significantly with their normal operational responsibilities or their responsibilities can be transferred or delegated effectively to others.

Yes ? No   4.   We are prepared to appropriately recognize and reward these people for their contributions in solving the problem.

Yes ? No   5.   If the answer to any of questions 1–4 is 'No', are we willing and/or able to do what is necessary to convert the answer to a 'Yes'?

Your answers to the preceding five questions will indicate the degree to which your organization is willing and/or able to develop your internal resources. A negative response to question 5 is a clear indication that you need outside assistance.

Checklist I.6
Is it possible to combine internal resources with external assistance?

The simple fact that your current internal resources are insufficient to deal effectively with a problem situation does not mean that they should be sidelined.

The following checklist will provide you with an indication of the degree to which your internal resources can and should be combined with external support.

Yes ? No   1. The problem is so technical that there is no justifiable reason to invest time and money to develop our internal competence.

Yes ? No   2. The problem is non-recurring and there is no ongoing internal need for the skills that the consultant will use to solve the problem.

Yes ? No   3. Someone is needed to temporarily fill a competency gap until members of our organization can gain the skills or find time to deal with the problem.

If you answer anything but 'Yes' to any of the preceding three questions, your best solution may be to actively involve your internal staff in combination with external consulting support.

WHAT TYPE OF CONSULTANT DO YOU NEED?

The following set of three checklists have been designed to help you to determine which of the five consultant types is most likely to be of value in a given problem situation. It is important that you go through these checklists in order. The first checklist in this section is designed to help you determine if your organization will be better served by Helping Hands or by one of the remaining three consultant types. The second narrows the choice down even further by helping you to decide if a Training Specialist or one of the two remaining consultant types is most appropriate. The third and final checklist will help you to choose between an Expert Consultant and a Process Consultant.

You will note that we have not included a checklist to help you decide if you need an Academic or not. Our reasoning is simple; we cannot think of any situations in which you need an Academic! We can, however, think of many reasons why they need you. That does not mean that you should avoid engaging a consultant simply because s/he is employed in an academic position at a university. It simply means that you should hire such individuals as a consultant, not as an Academic.

Checklist I.7
Do you need Helping Hands?

Instructions: Use the five point scale below to rate how well each of the five statements in this section describes the situation for which you are seeking consultant assistance:

5 = This statement is an **excellent description** of our current situation.
4 = This statement is a **good description** of our current situation.
3 = This statement is a **fair description** of our current situation.
2 = This statement is a **poor description** of our current situation.
1 = This statement **does not describe** our current situation **in any respect**.

5 4 3 2 1   1. What we need most is a strictly temporary addition to our existing workforce due to short-term demand for people with a specific set of skills and competencies.

5 4 3 2 1   2. The person that we bring in will be expected to fit into our existing workforce and function as a full- or part-time, but temporary 'producer'.

5 4 3 2 1   3. Someone in our organization will determine exactly what this person is expected to do and, to a large extent, how s/he is to do it.

5 4 3 2 1   4. Someone in our organization will actively supervise this person as s/he performs the task for which s/he was engaged.

5 4 3 2 1   5. This person's performance will be evaluated against the same standards that would be used to evaluate the performance of a permanent employee in the same position.

Total the points that you have given to each of the five statements above. In our judgement, a total of 22 or above is the only result that *clearly* indicates that a Helping Hands type of consultant is most appropriate for the assignment at hand. A total of less than 22 indicates that the organisation may be better served by one of the other three consultant types, in which case you can move on to the next checklist.

Checklist I.8
Do you need a Training Consultant?

The following checklist will help you to determine whether you need a Training Consultant or one of the remaining two consultant types.

Instructions: This checklist contains eight statements. As with the preceding checklist, your task is to use the five-point scale below to rate how well each statement describes the situation for which a consultant's assistance is being considered:

5 = This statement is an **excellent description** of our current situation.
4 = This statement is a **good description** of our current situation.
3 = This statement is a **fair description** of our current situation.
2 = This statement is a **poor description** of our current situation.
1 = This statement **does not describe** our current situation **in any respect**.

5 4 3 2 1   1. The primary cause of our problem situation is clearly a deficiency in knowledge, attitudes or skills.

5 4 3 2 1   2. Our organization has a well-defined need for the knowledge, attitudes and skills that are lacking, both now and in the future.

5 4 3 2 1   3. Individuals to be trained are likely to respond positively to an opportunity to learn the needed knowledge, attitudes or skills.

5 4 3 2 1   4. Individuals to be trained are likely to have little difficulty applying and utilizing their newly learned knowledge, attitudes and skills in the performance of their roles and job functions within our organization.

5 4 3 2 1   5. Our organization's management is prepared to take concrete steps to support, reinforce and reward individuals' efforts to apply the knowledge and skills gained from the training activity.

5 4 3 2 1   6. The training activity is unlikely to have any significant disruptive effects on other essential activities, functions or processes within our organization.

5 4 3 2 1   7.   A conscious decision has been made that the training act-
                  ivity is worth any temporary disruptions that it might cause.

5 4 3 2 1   8.   The costs of training individuals in the needed knowledge,
                  attitudes and/or skills is likely to be recouped in the form
                  of concrete increases in effectiveness or efficiency.

Total the points that you have given to each of the eight statements above.

In our judgement, the only result that *clearly* indicates that a Training Consultant
is most appropriate is a total of 37 or above. Any other result indicates that the services of one of the other two consultant types may be required. We must point
out, however, that a Training Consultant may be the best choice even with a total
of 30–36 points *if* the consultant selected is capable of and willing to help you and
participants to deal with the post-training issues indicated by statements 3–8.

   For example, one of the reasons for a lower points total may have been your
belief that your organisation cannot, at present, provide sufficient support, rein-
forcement or rewards to ensure the continued application of the knowledge and
skills taught (item 5). A Training Consultant may still be the best choice if s/he is
both willing and qualified to help you to develop an effective support system for
the training offered.

Checklist I.9
Do you need an Expert Consultant or a Process Consultant?

If your responses to the preceding two checklists did not convince you that a
Helping Hands or Training Consultant is what you need, you have only two
options remaining: an Expert Consultant or a Process Consultant.

Instructions: The following checklist differs in format from the previous two. It
contains twelve sections, each of which has two possible responses. Your task is
to distribute seven points between the two alternatives within each section.

   Use the seven points to indicate your sense of the relative importance of each of
the two options. For example, if you believe that option 'B' is considerably more
important than option 'A', your answer might look as follows:

   2   A
   5   B

In evaluating each pair of responses, reflect on the assignment for which the consultant is being considered. What do you want, need and expect the consultant to
do for you and your organization? What is best for your organization in both the

short and long term? What kind of working relationship do you want or need between the members of your organization and the consultant?

1. The nature of the problem:

———A.   This is a one-of-a-kind, non-recurring problem. Therefore, there is no advantage to our organization acquiring the competencies necessary to deal with similar problems in the future. As a result, our consultant will be expected to apply his/her specialized competencies to solve our problem for us.

———B.   The same or similar problems are likely to occur in the future. Therefore, it is essential that the consultant collaborate with management and others in our organization to solve the problem while simultaneously expanding and enhancing our internal ability to avoid and/or resolve similar problems in the future.

2. Determination of goals and methods:

———A.   Our organization's management should determine the goals to be achieved by our consultant, who will then be expected to determine the best methods for reaching these goals.

———B.   Our management and our consultant should work together in the determination of the goals to be achieved as the result of this consulting effort, and in identifying the best methods for achieving these goals.

3. Consultant–client relationship:

———A.   The nature of the relationship between management and our consultant is not important, as long as our consultant provides competent solutions to our problems through the application of his/her specialized skills and procedures.

———B.   The nature of the relationship between our management and our consultant is important because the consultant will be expected to actively collaborate with management throughout the consulting assignment.

4. Reporting

———A.   Our consultant should function primarily as a 'free agent', assuming primary responsibility for the successful completion of all stages of the consulting assignment.

———B.   Management and our consultant should share joint responsibility for the successful completion of the consulting assignment and should therefore maintain continual contact.

5. Control between management and our consultant:

———A.   Our consultant should have technical control over the project since s/he will be expected to have much more practical knowledge and experience in this area than the members of our organization. However, management should retain control over available resources and logistics.

———B.   Management should share control with our consultant by openly discussing and negotiating all issues that may emerge.

6. Situation analysis:

———A.   Our consultant should take full responsibility for analysing our problem situation. S/he should decide what information will be required, the methods to be used to gather it, from whom, and how it should be organized and analysed.

———B.   Management and our consultant should make *joint* decisions about what information will be required, the methods to be used to gather it, from whom, and how it should be organized and analysed

7. Conclusions and recommendations:

———A.   Our consultant should be responsible for deriving conclusions from his/her analysis of our problem situation and should use these as the basis for personally formulating and submitting concrete recommendations for improving/correcting our problem situation.

———B.   Management, key members of our organization *and* our consultant should work together to draw conclusions from the data collected and to formulate solutions to the problems identified.

8. Implementation of the problem solutions:

———A.   Our consultant's responsibility should end when s/he provides us with his/her recommendations for solving the problems at hand. If s/he is to be involved in the implementation process, it should be in the role of Expert Consultant with responsibility for implementing the technical side of solutions that s/he has developed.

———B.   Although our organization should take primary responsibility for implementing whatever solutions have been developed, our consultant should be expected to be actively involved in the implementation process. Our consultant's actual role may vary from that of 'coaching from the sidelines' to that of 'key player'. Whatever role s/he takes should be the result of open discussions between management and our consultant as the implementation plan is developed.

9. Managing disagreements:

———A.   Our consultant should be an expert in his/her field and the managers and members of our organization should show considerable respect for his/her competence. When disagreements occur between the views of our consultant and those of organizational members, it should be remembered that our consultant is very well paid for his/her opinions and knowledge.

———B.   Disagreements between organizational members and our consultant should be expected because of the differences in roles, responsibilities, backgrounds and interests. Both management and our consultant should view these differences as sources of potential innovation.

10. Acceptance of consultant recommendations:

———A.   Our consultant's recommendations are likely to meet with little resistance and are expected to be quickly and willingly implemented by organizational members.

———B.   Our consultant will be expected to help us to gain organizational acceptance of, support for and commitment to the problem solutions that s/he has recommended.

11. Evaluation of results:

———A.   A formal evaluation will take place at the conclusion of the consultation process for the primary purpose of determining if our consultant has delivered what s/he has promised.

———B.   Formal evaluations will be conducted throughout the consultation to determine if adjustments to recommended plans and strategies are necessary. These evaluations will cover such factors as (a) the progress being made, (b) the quality of the results being achieved and (c) the effectiveness of the plan and the methods being used.

12. Evaluators:

———A.   A. Management or someone assigned by management will evaluate the quality, relevance and effectiveness of the results produced by our consultant.

———B.   Management and our consultant will jointly evaluate the ongoing results of the consultation.

Scoring: Copy the values from each of the twelve sections of the preceding checklists to the scoring matrix below and total the scores in each column.

	Expert Consultant	Process Consultant
1.	A. ____	B. ____
2.	A. ____	B. ____
3.	A. ____	B. ____
4.	A. ____	B. ____
5.	A. ____	B. ____
6.	A. ____	B. ____
7.	A. ____	B. ____
8.	A. ____	B. ____
9.	A. ____	B. ____
10.	A. ____	B. ____
11.	A. ____	B. ____
12.	A. ____	B. ____
Totals:	A. ____	B. ____

A comparison of the totals in each of the above columns should indicate which of the two consultant types is likely to be most appropriate to assist you in resolving this problem situation. Although it is unlikely that the total points in any one of the two columns is zero, you will probably notice that you have given more points to one of the consulting types than to the other. For example, if you have given 60 points to Expert Consultants and only 24 to Process Consultants, you should attempt to ensure that the majority of the individuals on your short list of consultant candidates are Expert Consultants.

The greater the similarity between the points given to the two types of consultants, the more likely it is that the consultant you are looking for should have sufficient competence and flexibility to function in *both* modes of consultation. For example, it is not unusual to discover that what you need is a Process Consultant who is clearly able to function as an Expert Consultant *(and/or* as a Training Consultant or even as a Helping Hand) as the needs of your assignment dictate.

II

BUILDING CONSULTANT SELECTION CRITERIA

❖

3

IDENTIFYING PROFESSIONAL, ETHICAL CONSULTANTS

❖

Unprofessional, unethical consultant behaviour is costly! Aside from the measurable costs of wasted organizational resources, there are costs to you, the client, in terms of lost credibility within your own organization, increased difficulty generating commitment to future change efforts, losses in terms of damaged internal relationships, and so on. Such behaviour is also costly to those consultants who honestly attempt to perform their consulting responsibilities in a highly professional and ethical manner. We frequently encounter executives and managers who have been 'burned' by unethical consultants and, as a result, have difficulty trusting anyone who calls him/herself a consultant.

In this chapter we examine what we consider to be minimum standards for professional and ethical consultant behaviour. For convenience we discuss consultant professionalism and ethics as though they are two distinct categories of behaviour. However, you will note that there is considerable overlap and a close link between professionalism and ethics.

PROFESSIONAL CONSULTANT BEHAVIOUR

In our experience, truly professional consultants do seven things that clearly differentiate them from their less professional (hungrier!) colleagues:

1.   They treat the organization, not an individual, as the client.
2.   They focus on the root causes of the problem(s), not their symptoms.
3.   They focus on long-term effects, not on 'quick fixes'.
4.   They actively seek opportunities to develop and utilize your internal resources and competencies.
5.   They provide help to self-help in an effort to reduce your dependence on external assistance.

6.   They deal with practical reality.

7.   They maintain a helicopter perspective over the problem situation.

TREATING THE ORGANIZATION, NOT AN INDIVIDUAL, AS THE CLIENT

Many consultants unquestionably accept the notion that their 'client' is the senior person with whom they have negotiated their consulting contract and/or who authorizes the payment of their fees. Such consultants often feel obligated to satisfy the individual whom they perceive as their 'client'. We believe that consultants are, or at least, should be, hired and paid by organizations, not by individuals, implying that the consultant's primary task is to provide a service to the organization, not to an individual or group within the organization. The distinction between helping an individual 'client' and treating the organization 'as the client' is both a philosophical and an ethical issue.

Because the primary goal of any consulting effort should be to improve organizational conditions and performance, problems are likely to occur if the needs of the specific individual who engages the consultant are not in line with organizational needs. This is especially true if the consultant is expected to support or promote that individual's needs or goals at the expense of the organization's best interests. Take, for example, the case of the Director of a large service organization whose senior managers were strongly resisting his efforts to implement broad structural changes in the organization. He called in a consultant and tasked him with 'driving home' his intended changes, including identifying and reporting on any senior managers not actively supporting the change effort. The consultant could have easily accepted this assignment and, in return, received a considerable fee. But, to do so would probably have had an extremely negative long-term impact on the entire organization and would have perpetuated an unhealthy organizational norm of 'spying' on subordinates.

An additional risk, when consultants define an individual as their client, is that they also tend to orient their work around that individual's perceptions, beliefs, values, opinions and preferences. In such cases they may ignore the needs of other key individuals or groups within the organization or those of the organization's external stakeholders including suppliers, customers, financiers, regulators and stockholders.

One of the best ways to identify an unprofessional (or hungry) consultant is to explore the degree to which s/he is willing to allow your views of the situation to go unchallenged.

FOCUSING ON ROOT CAUSES, NOT THE SYMPTOMS OF PROBLEMS

Many clients already 'know' what they need to do in order to solve their problems. Unfortunately, their preferred solution is often based more on the symptoms of the problem than on its root causes. Part of a professional consultant's responsibility is to convince you to re-examine your conclusions and, if necessary, to help you to see the value of moving from 'needing what you want' to 'wanting what you need'.

Case in point

One of our colleagues was called in by a Marketing Director who opened the meeting by stating, 'We are receiving too many complaints about poor customer service. I want you to conduct a customer service course for all counter personnel.' The consultant suggested that she begin by interviewing a small group of counter personnel and customers to gain better insight into the nature of the problem and its causes. The Marketing Director rejected this step on the grounds that it would entail unnecessary extra time and costs; 'Just give me the course I'm asking for'. The consultant reluctantly agreed to design and conduct a course in customer service skills as demanded.

During the first customer service course, participants made it clear that they neither wanted nor needed training in customer service skills. In fact, they convinced the consultant that they were well aware of the elements of good service, that is, they knew what to do and how to do it. They perceived the course as too basic, redundant and unnecessary, and felt insulted that their management had requested such a course.

Counter personnel were also disappointed that their senior management had not cared enough to ask them what they saw as the causes of customer service problems. As they perceived it, the organization had very specific, strict rules that overly limited what they could and could not do to satisfy their customers. The penalties for 'breaking' these rules were severe. Even when common sense indicated that, in a specific transaction, a rule was inappropriate or unnecessarily restrictive, employees were compelled to follow it.

After the first course the consultant took her findings to the organization's Director, along with her suggestion that future customer service courses be suspended until the situation had been more carefully assessed. She further recommended that a team of counter personnel be formed and authorized to review current rules, regulations, policies and procedures governing their behaviour. This team would identify factors that they felt were causing customer service complaints and recommend modifications, additions or deletions. Senior management would review these recommendations and could accept, modify or reject them. The Director's response was to call the consultant 'insubordinate' and 'non-responsive' and replace her with a new, more compliant (hungrier and less competent) consultant who was willing to give him precisely what he wanted (despite the fact that it was not at all what he needed). Two years after the training programme provided by the new consultant, customer service in this firm had a reputation as 'the worst in the industry'.

Telling a prospective consultant which specific 'solution' you want him/her to implement can serve as a good test of the consultant's competence, courage and experience. The consultant who readily and unquestioningly offers to provide what you request may be unreliable. A truly professional consultant will say something like, 'before I accept your picture of the problem and its causes I'd like to develop my own picture of the situation. Is it all right if I talk with some of the people involved in or impacted by this problem?' Again, a consultant should not give you what you want; s/he should make sure that your organization gets what it really needs.

FOCUSING ON LONG-TERM EFFECTS, NOT 'QUICK FIXES'

A consultant's primary task is to improve the performance of your organization in the long run, not just the short run. Unfortunately, consultants often fall into the same trap as their clients; they focus too much of their energies on critical current problems and too little on attempting to prevent future problems from arising. Even when a consultant is called in to assist with a critical current problem, a significant portion of his/her attention and skills should be focused on helping the client system to avoid a recurrence of the same or similar problems in the future.

Case in point

The Russian Ministry for Atomic Power and Industry was having trouble dealing with conflicts between plant staff, between plants and the Ministry, and between the plants and environmental groups in the community. One of the authors was asked to join a group of specialists in conflict resolution to train Soviet psychologists to help them to resolve conflicts as they arose. All of the specialists selected were highly competent, both as conflict resolution experts and as Training Consultants. There was little doubt that the Soviet psychologists would, once fully trained, be able to step into a conflict and help to resolve it.

After several visits, the on-site author raised the question, 'After we run the last of our conflict resolution training programmes, what will we have contributed to the elimination, reduction or management of the *causes* of these conflicts in the long-term?' The conflict resolution specialists reluctantly agreed that the training they offered was not intended to be preventive, much less to provide 'early warning signals' for future conflict situations. It was restricted to effectively resolving conflicts once they become 'significant'. It was agreed that placing an equal or greater emphasis on training the Soviet psychologists in conflict prevention strategies and techniques would yield a far greater benefit in the long-term.

One of our favourite sayings as we work with executives is, 'When you are up to your butt in crocodiles, it's hard to remember that your primary responsibility is to drain the swamp.' One of the primary responsibilities of senior executives is to ensure that sufficient energy is committed to draining the swamp so that there will be fewer opportunities for crocodiles to breed and survive, thus reducing their number in the future. It is not easy to maintain a focus on draining the swamp when you are constantly being distracted by aggressive, ravenous crocodiles. A consultant's primary task is to help you drain your swamp. If s/he is too eager to grab a club and join you in beating the crocodiles, s/he is not the kind of consultant that you need.

DEVELOPING AND UTILIZING INTERNAL RESOURCES AND COMPETENCIES

There are very few situations in which your organization is totally lacking in the skills and competencies necessary to deal with critical issues and problems. Unfortunately, too many consultants are so concerned with the size of their consulting contract that they consciously or unconsciously avoid exploring the possibility of reducing their services by making efficient use of the competencies and resources that already exist within your organization. Some consultants seem to assume that because they are talking with you as a prospective client this is sufficient evidence that your organization does not have the staff competencies and resources needed to deal with the problems at hand. This extremely convenient assumption relieves such consultants of their responsibility for asking questions that might result in the discovery that your organization does not need their services at all.

A professional, confident consultant will ask questions such as: 'To what degree do your personnel already possess the competencies needed to deal effectively with this problem?', 'Where are they?', 'What can you/we do to mobilize them?', 'To what degree are they already committed to other vital activities?', and 'If competencies are lacking, can they be developed?' There are only two situations in which your organization should allow itself to become totally reliant on the services of an external consultant. The first is when the required skills, knowledge and/or staff are currently lacking and there is no need for these resources within your organization in the future. The second is when it would be more expensive in the long-term to utilize and/or develop internal skills, knowledge and/or staff than to employ an external consultant.

Case in point

An assessment of a large manufacturing firm indicated a very low level of cooperation and coordination between the firm's major departments. Follow-up interviews indicated that the firm's managers and supervisors had a number of good ideas for resolving many of the problems between them. As a result, selected managers and supervisors were formed into 'Problem Solving Task Forces' and given responsibility for 'developing concrete, practical recommendations for improving interdepartmental cooperation and coordination'. Skilled Process Consultants were made available to help the task forces form and function, but they did not involve themselves in the development of recommendations.

When the task forces presented their recommendations to senior management almost all were readily accepted as viable and practical. More importantly, the fact that the task forces were made up of representatives from different departments led to the 'spontaneous' reduction of many of the causes of poor cooperation and coordination. Task force members developed a better understanding of each other's needs and communicated that understanding to their co-workers outside of the task forces.

Clearly, an external Expert Consultant could have recommended tried-and-true ways to improve interdepartmental cooperation and coordination within the above organization. It is even possible, but not likely, that his/her solutions would have been more comprehensive or well structured than those developed by the various task forces. But there is no way that a consultant's recommendations could have been 'better' than those developed internally. The members of the task forces and, ultimately, their co-workers, were fully committed to ensuring the effective implementation of *their* recommendations because they felt a sense of ownership in the results of the process that they had participated in.

PROVIDING HELP TO SELF-HELP

Consultants have an ethical and professional responsibility to *work themselves out of a job whenever possible* and should be held accountable for transferring relevant skills, techniques and knowledge to the members of your organization. The transfer of the consultant's skills, knowledge and techniques to the members of your organization enables them to be more self-reliant and self-determining in the future. Further, and perhaps most important, it significantly reduces your organization's future dependence upon expensive external consultants. In fact, we believe that most consulting agreements should explicitly state that the consultants are expected to work with organizational members along two dimensions:

(1) helping your organization to achieve the intended results of the consulting effort and (2) enabling the members of your organization to achieve the same kinds of results by themselves, in the future.

We cannot leave this point without reporting on a situation that occurred as this book was being written. One of the authors brought up the issue of 'working yourself out of a job' during a meeting with a group of senior level management consultants. One of the consultants present became extremely agitated and stated, 'Hell, if every consultant tries to work himself out of a job there will be no work for management consultants in the future!' In some ways, he may be right; if every management consultant is sincerely interested in transferring skills, knowledge and technologies to the members of their client systems, there will be less opportunity for consultants to continue doing the same type of (outdated) work over the period of a consulting career. Instead they would be forced to continuously develop new and more effective skills, knowledge and technologies. Of course, this can only happen if clients *demand* that their consultants transfer applicable technologies to their organizations!

DEALING WITH REALITY

At times both authors of this book have been labelled 'enemies' of training. To some degree, this accusation is fully justified. We are strongly opposed to training activities that utilize artificial, irrelevant or synthetic methods such as case studies, roleplays and simulations in situations where there is plenty of readily available, relevant 'reality'. For example, an all too common approach to training is to send selected managers to public training courses, that is, courses that are open to participants from several different organizations. It is not surprising that in such courses many of the skills, situations and techniques presented are totally inappropriate and/or irrelevant to participants' back-home conditions and situations. One of our favourite one-liners is from an exceptionally honest Training Specialist in a public workshop who stated, 'half of what I'm going to teach you will turn out to be totally useless to you. The problem is, I don't know which half.'

To make matters worse, participants in public workshops are often the only representative from their organization or function attending the course. As a result they often find themselves isolated and without support when they attempt to apply their newly learned techniques in their 'back-home' situations. Their efforts to introduce newly learned ideas, concepts and skills to their workplaces are met with subtle or overt resistance. They may even be 'punished' when they try to demonstrate what they have learned and are often derided by being told, 'that crap you learned in "charm school" doesn't work in the real world'. In such cases it takes individual courage and dedication for returning participants to persist in trying to apply their learnings. No matter how good the public workshop and no matter how highly motivated the participants were, most give up attempting to use their new skills shortly after returning to their organizations.

A far better alternative to most public courses is to organize internal courses that provide participants with concepts, skills and techniques directly linked to their own 'real worlds'. For example, an in-house training workshop in problem-solving can be offered for intact work groups and begin with an assessment of the actual problems which participants are currently attempting to solve within their team/function. Participants can then be given training in solving these actual, real-life, work-related problems. They leave such workshops feeling more self-confident in their ability to utilize the newly acquired problem-solving concepts, skills and techniques when they resume their respective work responsibilities. Because they have a group of peers who share a common language, concepts, techniques and skills it is far more likely that they will cooperate with and support each other in the continued application of their learnings after programme completion.

MAINTAINING A HELICOPTER PERSPECTIVE

In most large, complex organizations changes in one part of the organization can have unexpected, often negative effects on other parts of the organization. We call this the 'clothesline effect'. Imagine a long clothesline filled with freshly washed clothes hanging to dry. Each garment is 'independent' in the sense that it is separate from other pieces of clothing on the line, just like the different units in an organization are independent. The garments are also linked together by the clothesline, just as organizational units and functions are, or should be, bound together by the organizational structure. On the clothesline, if you pull on one of the socks, the jockey shorts farther down the line jump. That is, there is inter-dependence between each of the items of clothing on the line, just as the departments and functions within an organization are interdependent. You cannot make significant changes in one department or element of an organization without precipitating a 'clothesline effect' in other organizational units or elements.

A qualified consultant should be able to help you to avoid or minimize the clothesline effect by ensuring that both you and s/he maintain a 'helicopter perspective' over your organization throughout the change effort. The need for a helicopter perspective is especially important and most often neglected by Expert Consultants who specialize in relatively narrow technical areas. They often 'forget' the existence of other key subsystems or processes within the organization. As a result, we find them recommending a new computer system without adequately considering the effects that system will have upon the individuals who will have to use it. Or, they recommend changes in the corporate structure without adequately considering the impact of the changes on organizational goals and values, employee morale, and so on.

By maintaining a helicopter perspective both you and your consultant will be better able to anticipate who or what is most likely to be affected by the changes being considered. As a result, you will be better able to proactively initiate measures intended to minimize possible negative effects and optimize the desirable results of the change effort. A helicopter perspective will also make it easier to identify which groups are critical to the change effort. That is, which groups, if they feel 'inconvenienced' by or uncommitted to the planned changes, are likely to interfere with or obstruct these plans. This will suggest which groups you should include early in a planned change process.

ETHICAL CONSULTANT BEHAVIOUR

The term 'ethical behaviour' is a foreign phrase to many of inhabitants of the consultant jungle. As a result, responsible consultants in many consulting specialities have formulated 'codes of ethical conduct' intended to guide the behaviour of consultants working within that speciality. Although these codes of conduct vary significantly from speciality to speciality, most deal with the following four elements:

O   maintaining confidentiality;
O   presenting realistic expectations;
O   avoiding conflicting assignments;
O   not recruiting from client organizations.

MAINTAINING CONFIDENTIALITY

During the Second World War there was a widely distributed series of posters that said, 'Loose Lips Sink Ships'. Loose consultant lips may not sink organizations, but they can most definitely cause considerable torpedo damage. Because of the nature of their work, consultants typically gain considerable information from and about their client organizations. Much of this information can be detrimental to you and/or to your organization if inappropriately spread by a consultant. It can also be very beneficial to the consultants and/or their firm if they choose to use it unethically or inappropriately in their work with other client organizations.

Many consultants 'innocently' break the ethical principle of confidentiality. For example, while attending the opening cocktail party at a professional conference one of the authors found himself cornered by a young consultant eager to brag about his accomplishments. About ten minutes into the one-way conversation the younger consultant said, 'Just to prove my point, I recently worked with XYZ Corp., helping them to develop their strategy for next year. With my help they have decided to . . .' After a couple of minutes the author interrupted and said, 'Excuse me, but are you aware that I have a client in direct competition with XYZ Corp., and you have already told me enough for me to thoroughly sabotage all the work that you have done for XYZ?'

Many consultants and consulting firms do not (or refuse to) see the relevance of our concerns about consultant confidentiality.

Case in point

We know of one large, very well known management consulting firm that is staffed by both chartered accountants and Expert Consultants. The (unpublished and carefully guarded) policy of this firm is that *all* information about *any* of their client organizations is to be made available to any of the firm's accountants or consultants upon request. In fact, many of this firm's consulting assignments come as the direct result of referrals from chartered accountants who, in the process of their accounting assignments, discover problem areas that could be addressed by a consultant. And, many of the chartered accountants' assignments come as the direct result of a referral from one of the firms' consultants. Unfortunately, this practice of 'you scratch my back, I'll scratch yours' goes far beyond the referral of clients between the accounting and consulting sides of the firm. It normally works something like this:

O   Management Consultant, Joe Doe, arranges for a first meeting with the Managing Director of a large petroleum company with whom he would like to consult.

O   In preparation for the meeting Joe browses through his firm's client database, which includes detailed information on every client organization that his firm's chartered accountants or consultants have worked with over the past five years.

O   Joe discovers that one of his firm's chartered accountants has been working with the petroleum company in which he is interested. He immediately calls the chartered accountant and is quickly provided with a complete summary of the petroleum company's confidential financial activities covering the past three years of operations.

O   Joe also discovers that one of his firm's consultants has been working with his prospective client's primary competitor. He contacts the consultant and a day later he has complete summaries of that project on his desk, including detailed reports on the assessed strengths and weaknesses of the competing firm.

O   From the reports Joe learns that his consulting colleague has been helping the senior management of the competing firm to develop a new vision and strategic plan. Joe makes an appointment for lunch with this consultant for the following day. By the time lunch is finished, Joe has a clear picture of the competitor's strategic plan for the next three years.

O   Thanks to the combined weight of all of the above, Joe is able to develop a comprehensive picture of his prospective client organization and its competitive environment. As a result, he is able to plan for and conduct an initial meeting that leaves his prospective client thoroughly impressed.

We cannot help but wonder how impressed the prospective client in the above case would be if he knew that other consultants within Joe's firm will have full access to Joe's data about his petroleum company when they prepare for meetings with competing petroleum companies in the coming months! One might also find reason to wonder how the prospective client's competitor would feel if they discovered that many of their professional secrets were being spread so freely.

PRESENTING REALISTIC EXPECTATIONS

It is only natural for highly stressed managers to want the consultant to provide them with a 'magic bullet'. Managers who are in critical need of consultative assistance are often quite vulnerable to unethical consultants willing to promise anything in order to get the assignment. And many consultants are often extremely skilful at telling their prospective client exactly what s/he wants to hear. This often takes the form of assurances that the intervention will be relatively quick, simple, painless and/or inexpensive, in addition to having a major positive impact on the organization's bottom-line.

Case in point

One of the most blatant examples of unrealistic, manipulative consultant promises is found in the standard practice of a well known international 'consulting' firm that we have encountered in the USA, UK, Europe and Africa. This firm promises to perform a comprehensive assessment of the organization's strengths and weaknesses 'at no fee'. All they ask in return is an opportunity to recommend solutions to any 'relevant' problems uncovered by their assessment. At the completion of the assessment, which can take as long as thirty to forty days in a large organization, the client is presented with a report that includes the 'discovery' of several major problems, which – surprise, surprise – are usually a perfect match to the consulting firm's capabilities.

The assessment report often concludes with a statement that the consulting firm is willing to 'guarantee' that the client organization will reap benefits that 'exceed the costs of the consulting intervention' as a direct result of following their recommendations. This guarantee is followed immediately by a qualification that it is only valid if the client (a) follows the exacting implementation requirements recommended and, of course, (b) allows the consulting firm to develop and implement the instruments by which the results of the change effort are evaluated!

There are two major ethical issues involved in the above case. First, no consulting firm, reputable or otherwise, can afford to conduct thirty days of assessment activities for free unless, of course, they are 100 per cent certain that they will be able to recoup their invested costs through a mammoth consulting assignment within the organization being assessed. The only way they can be certain of that is to know, in advance, what their assessment is going to 'reveal'. Second, there is only one way that a consulting firm can guarantee its results and that is if it has full control over the evaluation of those results. No matter how experienced or competent the consultant may be, the simple fact is that there are far too many possible variables between the inception and the final evaluation of a change effort and the consultant does not, and should not, have control over most of these variables.

AVOIDING CONFLICTING ASSIGNMENTS

At times it is easy for the consultant to determine that two consulting assignments are in conflict with each other. For example, one of the authors recently assisted the management of a large corporation in developing their competitive strategy for the coming five years. Shortly afterwards he was approached by his client's toughest competitor and asked to do similar work for them. Clearly these two assignments would have been conflicting, that is, it would have been impossible for the consultant not to be influenced by the 'inside' knowledge he had obtained from the previous client, even if his intentions were 'pure'.

At other times it is more difficult to determine the degree to which two assignments are potentially conflicting. For example, the same author was responsible for designing and facilitating an extremely successful management development programme for a large manufacturing company. Several months after the completion of the programme he was contacted by the Managing Director of a competing company who wanted 'a similar management development programme' for his management team and senior staff. In this case even the author was uncertain of the degree to which this situation would be seen as a conflict of interest by his previous client. As a result, he discussed the situation openly with the management of both organizations to ensure that there were no misunderstandings.

NOT RECRUITING FROM CLIENT ORGANIZATIONS

It is clear that a consultant's job is to help you to improve the effectiveness of your organization, not to decrease that effectiveness by raiding your most effective employees. Therefore, we view consultants who serve, officially or unofficially, as 'headhunters' for their client organizations as unethical. For example, we would severely question a consultant who tells a client something like, 'When I was doing a job for XYZ company they had a young engineer who is just what you need in your organization. How about if I talk to him and see if he is interested in talking with you?' Some consultants attempt to salve their conscience in such situations by saying, 'Of course, it would be unethical for me to arrange the contact between you and this individual. Instead, I will give you his/her name and you can make the contact yourself.'

CHAPTER SUMMARY

The specific professional and ethical standards that guide the consultant you engage must, to a large degree, complement your own philosophy and values and those of your organization. Therefore you, as the prospective client, have both the right and the duty to question prospective consultants regarding their overriding values and standards. Once you have determined the level of professional and ethical behaviour that you require, don't accept a consultant who offers you anything less!

4

CONSULTANT SKILLS, EXPERIENCE AND PERSONAL CHARACTERISTICS

❖

Professional, ethical behaviour will provide a consultant with a solid foundation for doing a good job. However, it is of little value if the consultant lacks the skills, experience and/or personal characteristics necessary to help you to resolve your specific problem(s). In this chapter we provide you with a list of the competence, experience and personal characteristic factors that you should look for in a consultant, along with some specific tips on how to explore them with a consultant candidate.

CONSULTING SKILLS

You may have heard it said that 'consulting is not a skill, it is an art'. That statement usually comes out of the mouths of individuals who have never had the opportunity, time or interest to attend a professionally run consultant training programme. In many ways skilled consultants are like very talented artists. No matter how much conceptual talent they possess, if they haven't mastered the skills and techniques necessary to put what they 'see' onto canvas, they will not produce pictures of any value.

It is not easy to judge a consultant's competence in advance. All too often the only measure readily available to you is how much they charge. The implication is that the higher the fee, the more skilled the consultant. For example, one of the authors missed out on a consulting assignment recently because the fee he requested was 25 per cent *less* than the fee requested by a competing consultant. When asked why she had chosen the competing consultant, the client replied, 'on paper you both seemed to be equally qualified, but with the fee the other consultant requested we figured that he must be better than you'. (The fact that the author had personally trained the selected consultant only added to his feeling of having salt poured into an open wound!)

Obviously, higher consulting fees do not automatically mean higher competence. Some consultants set their fees on the basis of 'what the traffic will bear', others on the basis of what they think is 'fair value' for the services rendered. But if you can't judge a candidate's competence by the size of the fees s/he charges, what should you look at? There are three areas that you should examine in your efforts to determine the competency of a prospective consultant: (1) technical competence, (2) consulting competence, and (3) interpersonal competence.

TECHNICAL COMPETENCE

Technical competence is the most difficult of the three types of competencies to assess. With the exception of Helping Hands, consultants are usually expected to provide knowledge and specialized skills that are currently lacking within your organization - and if your organization does not have the sought-after competence, it may be difficult to recognize if the consultant has it.

Case in point

In the mid-1980s one of the authors came to the inevitable conclusion that it was time to computerize his consulting firm. Because he knew absolutely nothing about computers the author did what the adverts suggest; he let his fingers do the walking and contacted a 'consultant' who marketed himself in the yellow pages as an 'expert in computer systems for small professional firms'. The consultant behaved as one would expect a qualified Expert Consultant to behave. He asked a lot of questions and appeared to listen carefully to the answers. A week later he presented detailed written recommendations which, unfortunately, included a lot of strange words like megabytes, extended memory, expanded memory, rams, coprocessors and VGAs. The author was too ashamed to admit to the consultant that he had no idea what these words meant! Instead, he nodded knowingly and bought the entire package recommended by the Expert Consultant.

It took several weeks to discover that the 'solution' he had purchased was totally inappropriate to the needs of his organization. In fact, the computer he purchased utilized a little known operating system that was totally incompatible with either of the two standards that were predominant at the time, Mac or IBM. The 'Expert Consultant' was nothing more than a skilled salesman desperate to unload a warehouse full of what he knew to be lemons.

The process of judging a prospective consultant's technical competence for a given assignment is made even more complex by the fact that the skills expected of one consultant type are likely to differ significantly from those expected of another type of consultant:

O   Helping Hands must have technical competence in the specific tasks that they are being employed to perform.

O   Expert Consultants must have a high level of technical competence in their own speciality.

O   Training Specialists must not only have technical competence in their own speciality, but must also be proficient in the methodologies of adult education (androgogy).

O   Process Consultants are not usually expected to possess technical competence. Instead, they should be experts in generating and effectively managing appropriate organizational, intergroup, group, interpersonal and personal dynamics.

As far as we know, there are no 'guaranteed' methods for assessing a consultant's technical competence. There are, however, four techniques that can help you make the process somewhat more rational. The first is to gather your managers and key staff for an open discussion around the topic 'What do we lack in the way of the technical competence required to manage this problem ourselves?' The answer to this question will tell you what specific categories of technical skills the consultant you select must possess in order for him/her to be of most benefit.

A second technique is to ask prospective consultants the following three questions:

1.   Based on your understanding of our problem, what technical competencies do you believe are needed to deal with our situation?

2.   To what degree do you, personally, possess these competencies?

3.   How can you prove that you do, in fact, possess the competencies that you claim to possess?'

A third method is to request that the consultant provide you with a list of references from specific individuals who can verify his/her technical competence in areas directly related to the consulting assignment for which s/he is being considered.

A fourth method is to suggest, or ask the consultant to suggest, some form of pilot activity through which his/her technical competence can be tested.

Again, none of the above methods will provide you with definitive proof that a consultant has the technical competence required for the tasks to be performed – but at least they will increase your odds of making the best choice.

CONSULTING COMPETENCE

Technical competence alone is not sufficient to ensure that a consultant will be capable of providing the requested services at the requisite level or that these services will yield expected results. We know of many 'consultants' who appear to possess a high degree of technical knowledge or skill but are unable to use that knowledge and skill as the basis for effectively consulting with, facilitating and/or developing others. In addition to technical competence a skilled consultant must also be adept at applying a set of basic consulting competencies. The basic consulting competencies that are most often required in order to help individuals, groups and organizations to change include a high degree of competence in the following areas:

O   **Analysis and diagnosis:** The ability to select, collect, sort and analyse information from relevant sources related to the problem(s) to be solved. This competency includes the ability to identify and distinguish between the symptoms and root causes of a problem.

O   **Strategic planning:** The ability to help key members of a client organization to formulate, agree on and commit to a 'desired state' and to identify and select from alternative strategies for reaching that state.

O   **Change management:** The ability to help organizations and their members to effectively plan for, implement, manage and monitor change, including a high degree of skill in effectively managing the dynamics of adoption of and resistance to change at the individual, group and organizational levels.

O   **Evaluation:** The ability to develop and implement valid strategies for identifying and evaluating the intended and unintended results of the consulting services provided.

Obviously, not all assignments require a consultant with a high degree of competency in all of the preceding skill areas. It is up to you to decide the minimum level of competence required of the consultant in your specific problem situation.

INTERPERSONAL COMPETENCE

In addition to technical and consulting competence, most consulting assignments demand that the consultant be competent in managing relationships, interactions and transactions with others. The most essential interpersonal competencies required of a consultant include: confrontation skills, risk-taking skills, collaboration, conflict management skills and relationship building skills.

Confrontation skills

At times it may be necessary for a consultant to say things to you or to the members of your organization that may be 'unpleasant'. For example, it may be necessary to tell one of your more senior executives that his/her behaviour is one of the primary causes of the problem that the consultant has been engaged to help solve. The consultant may also be required to 'point out the dead moose in the boardroom', that is, bring to the surface an issue that everyone knows exists (because they keep tripping over its festering, stinking bulk) but no one dares to acknowledge, much less openly confront. Openly confronting problems may seem like an obvious part of the consultant's job. Yet, we frequently encounter consultants who avoid confronting influential members of their client organizations with uncomfortable truths, usually because they fear that it will result in the reduction or cancellation of their consulting contract.

Risk-taking skills

There is almost always a degree of real or perceived risk in organizational problem-solving and change. For the members of the organization, the risks may include the fear of leaving familiar ground, the fear that someone might get 'hurt' if sensitive issues arise, the fear of being discovered as less than competent, and so on. For the consultant, the risks might include, for example, the fear of the impact of unpopular recommendations, and the fear of trying a relatively unproved method. A consultant may also share organization members' fear of confronting a powerful executive who is perceived as likely to respond negatively. Competent consultants do not allow themselves to be paralysed by their own fears or the fears of organizational members. They know that such fears are natural and normal. More importantly, they know that their fears must be managed appropriately as part of their consulting role and that true courage is doing what has to be done, even though one is aware and afraid of the potential negative consequences.

When screening consultant candidates it is often useful to ask them to provide examples of significant risks that they have taken in their consultant role. Those who cannot provide you with concrete examples may be too cautious (or dishonest) to be of any real value to you or your organization. If the consultant readily provides many examples but seems inordinately pleased with his/her survival skills you should probe further to assess what s/he would consider to be an 'acceptable risk'. If the consultant's definition of *acceptable* exceeds yours, scratch him/her off your short list and move on.

Collaboration

Consulting is not something that consultants do in isolation. It is, or at least should be, done in collaboration with the managers, leaders and members of your organization and, occasionally, in collaboration with your organization's customers, suppliers and other stakeholders. A consultant who has difficulty cooperating and collaborating with others, who is likely to compete with your managers or other members of your organization and/or may otherwise attempt to achieve undue prominence is likely to have little positive and, possibly, a great deal of negative impact on your organization. The same is true of a consultant who remains inaccessible or remote from those with whom s/he should be working. An effective consultant is flexible, seeks ways to enable organizational members to satisfy their needs and preferences and clearly demonstrates a willingness to 'share the spotlight' with others. However, *collaborative* is not synonymous with *compliant*. Good consultants will not compromise their professional integrity to avoid unpleasant conflicts or necessary confrontations.

Conflict management

Some people perceive the word *conflict* as synonymous with the words *quarrel, feud* and/or *argument*. In our view a *conflict* is something that occurs whenever two or more 'things' occupy the same space at the same time, such as when the goals, priorities, interests, positions, needs, preferences and/or desires of one individual or group differ from those of another individual or group. In other words, a conflict can be as insignificant as two people needing the same computer terminal at the same time or as serious as two department managers competing for scarce resources. Conflict within an organization is both natural and inevitable. More importantly, appropriately managed conflicts are the basis of innovative and synergistic problem solutions.

Conflicts can arise at any time during a consulting effort. They can occur during your first meeting with a prospective consultant, focused on differences between what you think you want and what the consultant thinks that you need. They can also occur during the data gathering phase as some members of your organization question the consultant's right or need to gather certain information. And they can occur during the implementation phase when powerful members of your organization disagree about strategies or methods for achieving desired changes. Whenever they arise, the consultant's job is to manage them as effectively as possible, and that takes skill.

An effective consultant is skilled at managing at least two types of conflict situations. One is conflict in which the consultant is personally involved; for example, if an influential member of your organization demands that the consultant acts in a way that s/he considers to be unprofessional and/or unethical. The other is the situation in which the consultant is called in as a neutral, objective 'third party' to help individuals and/or groups within your organization to manage their legitimate differences.

Some consultants seem to be more skilled at creating than at resolving conflicts. That may be acceptable in situations where conflicts can be used to generate innovative thinking, but beware of consultants who seem to thrive on antagonizing others. Other consultants seem to prefer avoiding conflicts, by either pretending that conflicts don't exist or minimizing their potential consequences. Again, that may be valuable in some situations, but the most common result is that the conflict returns in a more intense form at some time in the future or that it gets fought 'behind closed doors'.

We strongly recommend that you look for a consultant who is skilled at managing and utilizing conflicts. Such consultants will help the members of your organization to turn potentially negative conflicts into synergistic, win–win situations. The concept of 'win–win' solutions is an important one to keep in mind. Too many consultants (and managers) seek and/or willingly accept compromise solutions, where each party in the conflict gives a little of what s/he wants and/or needs in order to satisfy the needs of the other party. Such solutions are usually 'lose–lose', that is, where both parties feel that they have lost something as part of the negotiated compromise. A true 'win-win' solution is one in which both parties come out feeling fully satisfied with the agreement reached. Although such agreements are typically much more difficult to arrive at than compromise solutions, they are almost always possible, and usually much longer lasting.

Case in point

Many years ago one of the authors was asked to help a young couple to resolve a conflict that was severely damaging their marriage. The husband was an avid outdoorsman who wanted to spend all three weeks of their holidays hunting and fishing. The wife hated tents and the accompanying pests. For her the ideal holiday was at a luxury resort. During the early years of their marriage the couple tried to compromise. They spent half of their holidays in the mountains where the wife was miserable and half in seaside resorts where the husband was miserable. The past two years they had taken separate vacations, which only increased the animosity between them and made their relationship even worse.

The author asked each of the two what they wanted most from their holidays. The husband said he wanted physical exercise in fresh air, closeness to nature, good fishing and hunting, a chance to be alone, and so on. The wife said that she wanted to be 'pampered', closeness to shopping, and good food prepared for her. The author suggested that instead of arguing or compromising, the couple seek a place that met both of their needs. The answer was found in Lake Tahoe, Nevada, which is a mountain resort where the husband could spend his days communing with nature while his wife lazed by the pool or went shopping. In the evening they enjoyed a wide choice of restaurants and entertainment which both of them enjoyed.

Relationship building

A consultant's effectiveness is likely to be dependent upon his/her ability to establish and maintain trusting relationships with the managers and members of your organization. Although relationship building is essential throughout a consulting effort, it is especially important (1) as the consultant works with you to formulate the goals and direction of the consulting project, and (2) as the consultant gathers diagnostic data from the members of your organization.

Perhaps the most critical aspect of a productive consulting relationship is trust. The less the management and members of your organization trust the consultant, the less likely they are to open up and reveal the range and depth of information needed in order to help them to deal effectively with relevant organizational issues. Trust means a sense that the consultant can and will do what s/he promises. There is no sure way of determining, in advance, if the consultant will be trustworthy. The most you can expect from your first meeting with a prospective consultant is an indication of his/her trustworthiness.

It can take considerable time for a consultant to earn a sufficient degree of trust from the key members of your organization. Until that trust is earned, you and your senior managers may have to operate on 'faith'. Once earned, it may take no time at all for that trust to be lost. One of the quickest ways for a consultant to lose a client's trust is to mishandle the issue of confidentiality, as illustrated in the following case.

Case in point

A consultant had promised participants in a management workshop that any information that came up during the workshop would be treated confidentially. The consultant stated specifically that he would not divulge his perceptions of participant skill levels to anyone outside of the training group. Shortly after the workshop the consultant was talking casually with the organization's CEO over lunch. The CEO stated that she was considering promoting one of the course participants, X, to a senior management position. The consultant spontaneously stated, 'If I were you I would wait awhile before promoting X. He is very good, but needs a few more months of development in his current position before he is ready for more responsibility. I suggest that you promote Y instead.' Word quickly spread throughout the organization that the consultant had broken his promise of confidentiality and that X had not been promoted over Y as a result. Needless to say, the quality of participation and openness in management training workshops conducted by this consultant quickly sank to an unacceptable level and it became necessary to replace him.

Before leaving the above case we want to point out that we do not consider it to be inherently wrong for a consultant to share his/her perceptions of individual members of a client organization with the leaders of that organization. This is perfectly valid consultant behaviour *if* the consultant and organizational members have discussed the issue and have agreed on what the consultant may and may not talk about outside of a workshop or meeting. It is, however, *absolutely unethical* for a consultant to discuss individuals when s/he has promised confidentiality.

EXPERIENCE

You must determine how specifically related the consultant's past experience ought to be in relation to the issues to be dealt with. There are three types of consulting experience that you should consider in developing your consultant selection criteria:

1.   Experience with similar types of problems.
2.   Experience at a specific organizational level.
3.   Experience with similar organizations and/or industries.

Is it sufficient that the consultant has considerable experience with similar problems, such as being an expert in conflict management? Or, does your situation require a consultant with specific experience working at a specific level of the organization, for example, helping to manage and utilize conflicts within executive committees? A third option is that the consultant must be skilled at working within a specific industry or type of organization; for instance, we know of a consultant who specializes in conflicts between doctors and nurses.

There are several things to consider in determining the breadth or focus of the experience that you should demand of the consultant that you select. In general, a consultant who has never worked with the senior management of a large organization may lack the perspective and self-confidence necessary to help your senior management to design and implement an organization-wide change effort. A consultant who has never worked with lower level workers, supervisors and middle managers may not appreciate how people at these levels are likely to perceive and react to changes being promoted by senior management.

Consultants who are intimately familiar with one type of industry are often better able to provide in-depth recommendations to specific problems. However, such consultants may miss critical pieces of information because they inappropriately assume that conditions in your organization are the same as those that they had experienced in similar previous client systems. A consultant less experienced in your specific industry may ask 'dumb' or naïve questions – and it may be just such questions that help you to discover and examine holes in your own assumptions about the organization.

Although experience is an extremely important criterion in selecting a consultant, a consultant's capacity to learn from experience is far more important than the experience itself. Very often, highly experienced consultants become complacent and rely on formulas and methods they developed in the past for different people and different organizations operating under different conditions. A bright, curious, intuitive, less experienced consultant may be more effective than a highly experienced consultant who has stopped learning or caring.

The depth or focus of experience that you require of a consultant may also depend on the type of consultant that you are seeking. If your organization needs an Expert Consultant or a Training Specialist, the consultant you select should probably have very specific, in-depth experience with the specialized organizational issues to be dealt with. On the other hand, if you need a Process Consultant, specific experience with the technical aspects of the problem may be less important and even a handicap.

An effective method for identifying how much experience and of what type(s) a consultant should have is to develop and agree on a comprehensive list of your requirements in each of the three areas: experience with similar problems, experience in working at specific organizational levels, and experience in similar organizations and industries.

PERSONAL CHARACTERISTICS

While it is important to consider how a consultant works and what competencies and experience s/he possesses, it is equally important to consider who the consultant 'is' as a person. The factors that we consider most essential in evaluating a consultant's personal characteristics are:

- O   core values,
- O   self-confidence,
- O   results orientation,
- O   ability to manage personal needs, and
- O   ability to manage personal style preferences.

CORE VALUES

To appreciate fully the importance of identifying a potential consultant's core values, consider what would happen if you engaged a chauvinistic male consultant to help your organization become less discriminatory towards female employees. Or, if you hire a consultant biased towards autocratic, centralized management to assist you in the creation of a more transparent, empowering organizational culture.

If your organization is or may soon be involved in sensitive social issues, it is in your own interest to spend a significant amount of time exploring a prospective consultant's core values, including the degree to which these values fit and complement the prevailing or intended values of your organization.

SELF-CONFIDENCE

An appropriate degree of self-confidence is a critical asset for a consultant. However, an overly self-confident consultant may take on more responsibility than s/he can professionally handle. If they are perceived as arrogant, their attitude may increase rather than decrease resistance to solving the problem. In such cases, it may be useful to ask the candidate about the basis of their high opinion of themself. On the other hand, a consultant who lacks self-confidence may avoid taking necessary risks out of fear of failure. S/he may also have difficulty 'selling' ideas to key members of your organization.

It is often easy to misjudge a consultant candidate's true level of self-confidence. Inexperienced consultants may try to compensate for a short résumé by affecting a façade that exudes self-confidence. Alternatively, many highly competent consultants are fairly conservative and even humble in their presentations of their experience and capabilities, which can easily be misinterpreted as having low self-confidence. One way to explore a prospective consultant's level of self-confidence is to ask him/her to tell you a bit about their strengths and weakness. If s/he responds with nothing but strengths, be on guard; s/he may only be trying to impress you or s/he may have little or no awareness of his/her own weaknesses. Either way, s/he may not be the consultant you want. You should also be on guard if s/he seems reluctant or unable to tell you about his/her strengths, or seems better able to tell you about his/her weaknesses. This consultant may lack the self-confidence necessary to do the job. The consultant you are looking for is the one who is able to provide a list of significant strengths without appearing to brag, and a list of areas in which s/he needs improvement without appearing apologetic.

RESULTS ORIENTATION

Effective consultants are often results-oriented individuals. That is, they have an innate need to set and achieve both short- and long-term goals for their activities. As a result, they dislike working against such 'soft' targets as *resolving conflict, improving teamwork* or *modifying the structure*. For such consultants these phrases are far too ambiguous to offer the sense of achievement that they need when working on an assignment. What they usually require, as individuals, are (1) a set of clear, concise mileposts so that they can measure their progress, and (2) clearly defined overall goals for the project so that they know when they have arrived. If either goals or mileposts are lacking in a project, results-oriented consultants will tend to create them for themselves.

Your challenge is to ensure that the consultant that you engage is (1) sufficiently results-oriented to establish a sense of urgency to the work that s/he does, but (2) not so results-oriented that they move too rapidly or take too many unnecessary risks to meet their own internal needs for achievement. The best way to assess the degree to which your consultant candidates are results-oriented is to ask them to tell you about one or two of their most recent consulting assignments. The consultant that you want will proudly describe the degree to which they met concrete goals and mileposts set for the assignments that they have been involved in. The consultants that you don't want are those who focus their description on what they did during the assignment, such as, 'we did a teambuilding (restructuring, strategic plan, and so on)', but seems unclear about the specific output related results of the activities that they conducted. You should also beware of consultants who frequently begin statements in their description with 'I did . . .'. Such consultants are often so results-oriented that they may leave you and other members of your organization in their dust as they eagerly rush forward to challenge new boundaries of performance.

ABILITY TO MANAGE PERSONAL NEEDS

Consultants are (or at least should be) human beings and, as such, have their own needs, problems and interests. In fact, any consultant who denies that many of his/her personal needs are satisfied as a direct result of working with clients is likely to be lacking in adequate self-awareness, or is blatantly lying. However, a consultant's personal needs and/or problems should never be allowed to interfere with his/her performance. In addition to being both unprofessional and unethical, such behaviour can easily reduce and even destroy the positive effects of the consulting assignment. You, as a prospective client, have a right to ask questions aimed at assessing consultant candidates' awareness of their own needs, including their capability to manage these needs as they work within your organization.

Two areas of personal needs that can be most difficult for a consultant to manage, and most hazardous to you if they don't manage them, are the consultant's needs (1) for power and influence and (2) for close personal contact. Consultants with exceptionally high needs to have influence over others may consciously or unconsciously attempt to take over responsibility for the change effort instead of ensuring that responsibility for the effort remains in the hands of managers and members of your organization. Consultants with exceptionally high needs to be influenced by others may be too easy for you or the members of your organization to 'walk over'. Consultants with high needs for close personal contact with others may be unwilling to take risks that might endanger their relationship with you and/or other members of your organization. Consultants with low needs for close personal contact with others may have difficulty developing the types of relationships necessary to function effectively. They may appear cool, distant, aloof and inaccessible. As a result, people who could benefit from their contributions may not be willing to initiate contact.

Again, your tasks as a client are (1) to discover the relative strength of consultant candidates' personal needs in any area that you believe may be important to the assignment for which they are being considered; (2) the degree to which they are aware of their own needs in each area; and (3) the degree to which they are able to ensure that their own needs do not inappropriately interfere with their role as a consultant.

ABILITY TO MANAGE PERSONAL STYLE PREFERENCES

There is a saying that 'either you have *it*, or you don't'. While we agree that there is an *it* that most highly effective consultants possess, we have difficulty defining what *it* is. The difficulty may lie in the fact that the prerequisite *it* differs from consultant to consultant. Instead of advising you to seek a consultant with *it*, we recommend that you begin by defining what you expect that the consultant's *it* should be for the assignment at hand.

Case in point

Many years ago one of the authors had taken a day off to work in his garden. Early that afternoon he received a panicky call from his secretary informing him that the Human Resources (HR) and Training Directors of a major farm tractor manufacturing firm had just called to see if they could 'drop by for a visit' with the consultant. The secretary knew that the consultant had been trying for several months to arrange a meeting with these men, so she had invited them to the office. They were scheduled to arrive in an hour. When he received the call from his secretary the consultant was knee deep in what might most politely be described as 'bovine excrement'. He weighed the choices of showering and changing clothes, thereby arriving late for the meeting or going to the office as he was. He chose the latter option and arrived for the meeting wearing old cowboy boots, well-worn jeans, a rather raggedy flannel shirt and a very distinctive cologne (a blend of Old Spice and Old Stockyard). The two visitors were wearing three-piece suits, white shirts and ties.

Twenty minutes into the meeting both visitors had removed their coats and ties. An hour later they had unbuttoned their waistcoats and two hours later the HR Director had removed his shoes. At the end of the meeting they awarded the consultant the largest contract in his career to that point in time. A couple of months later the consultant and the HR Director were joking about their first meeting and the consultant's appearance. The HR Director confessed, 'Son, that's exactly why we gave you the contract; you were the only consultant we interviewed who looked like he could understand us tractor-folk!'

In the case above, the HR Director recognized that the consultant had the *it* that he was looking for. But, had the HR Director represented a major bank or computer manufacturer, he may well have (mentally or physically) walked out of the first meeting, unless, of course, he too had grown up among the delightful scents and fragrances of a farm.

INTRODUCTION TO PART II CHECKLISTS

In this and the preceding chapter we provided you with a foundation for developing a selection criteria against which you can compare the consultants that you interview. The checklists that follow are intended to help you to develop and agree on your final checklist and to use it to your best advantage.

PART II
CHECKLISTS

❖

CONSULTANT SELECTION CRITERIA

In this section we present several relatively general checklists intended to serve as the foundation upon which you can build your own specific, detailed consultant selection criteria. These criteria will be used to evaluate the consultants that you are considering for a given assignment.

Because the checklists in this section are general, they cannot be used in their present form. To make them more specific, you and other influential members of your organization must:

○   identify the specific factors that should be included in your consultant selection criteria for this specific assignment;
○   ensure that you have a common definition of each factor; and
○   determine the relative importance of each factor.

If time allows, we strongly recommend that you initially work individually as you prepare for your discussion of the above three tasks. That is, each person involved in developing your selection criteria should individually review your general checklists; adding, deleting or modifying factors as s/he sees fit. Then each individual should develop his/her own personal definition of each factor before rating its importance as a selection criterion.

As you and your senior management begin with discussing the checklists we suggest that you first focus upon why each factor on your sample checklists is important. Observe that we said 'why' is this factor important, not 'is it' important. A discussion over 'is it important' is a closed-ended, 'yes/no' debate. Focusing on 'why is it important' will lead to an open-ended discussion that should clarify and elaborate the usefulness of each factor. This discussion may also lead to the identification of additional factors that were not on your original individual lists.

As you seek agreement on the factors to be included on your final list, a simple rule should be, if you can't justify including a factor, take it off the list!

To help you with your discussion, we have provided a four-point scale on all checklists that you can use to rate the degree of importance of each factor relevant to the consultant that you select for this assignment:

4 = This is a **critical characteristic** which the consultant must clearly demonstrate.

3 = This is an **important characteristic** which the consultant should demonstrate.

2 = It would be beneficial if the consultant has this characteristic, **but not essential**.

1 = The consultant **need not have this characteristic**.

Checklist II.1
Professional consultant behaviour

---

4 3 2 1   1. **Treat the organization as the client**: Our consultant must be well aware that his/her primary task is to improve the effectiveness of our organization, not merely to serve the needs of a specific individual or group; s/he must be willing and able to confront powerful organization members whose actions s/he perceives as counter to our organization's best interest.

4 3 2 1   2. **Focus on the root causes of problems**: Our consultant must have the courage to insist that we re-examine and, if necessary, redefine our perception of the problem situation to ensure that we get what we need, not just what we want; s/he must be willing and able to patiently surface and properly evaluate possible root causes of our problem as opposed to jumping in the direction of readily apparent solutions.

4 3 2 1   3. **Focus on long-term effects**: Our consultant must be willing and able to help us to avoid quick fixes; s/he must have a clear focus on 'draining the swamp' and be clearly interested in helping us to avoid a recurrence of the same or similar problems in the future.

4 3 2 1   4. **Develop and utilize internal resources**: Our consultant must be clearly interested in helping us to reduce our current and future dependence on external consulting resources by helping us to more effectively identify, train, mobilize, utilize and manage our internal problem-solving resources whenever appropriate.

4 3 2 1 5. **Provide help to self-help**: Our consultant must be clearly guided by the principle of working him/herself out of a job and be willing to be held accountable for transferring relevant skills, techniques and knowledge to the members of our organization, thus increasing our ability to effectively deal with similar problems in the future.

4 3 2 1 6. **Focus on practical reality**: Our consultant must be willing and able to create an environment which maximizes our use of reality to ensure that our change process is relevant, realistic and applicable; s/he must be capable of identifying and implementing activities that increase the probability that the members of our organization take ownership of the change effort and responsibility for its successful continuation after our consultant's departure.

4 3 2 1 7. **A helicopter perspective**: Our consultant must be willing and able to help us to avoid or minimize possible clothesline effects from this change effort by ensuring that we and s/he maintain a systems view; s/he must be alert to and able to deal with unexpected, often negative effects of his/her activities on other parts of our organization.

Checklist II.2
Ethical consultant behaviour

4 3 2 1 1. **Maintaining confidentiality**: Our consultant must be willing and able to treat confidential data coming into his/her care in the course of a consulting assignment with integrity.

4 3 2 1 2. **Presenting realistic expectations**: Our consultant must be willing and able to provide realistic, attainable goals and objectives for this assignment; s/he must ensure that our management and others involved in this effort are aware of predictable or likely risks and downsides of measures taken to resolve our problem and be prepared to help us to effectively eliminate or reduce damage caused by unforeseeable risks.

4 3 2 1 3. **Avoiding conflicting assignments**: Our consultant must be willing and able to proactively scan our internal and external environments and quickly identify, report and discuss any

potential conflicts of interest related to the existing or future assignments.

4 3 2 1   4. **Not recruiting**: Our consultant must be willing and able to demonstrate to our satisfaction that they are unlikely to use their position within our organization to identify and recruit staff for other organizations.

Checklist II.3
Technical competence

Our organization is currently lacking the following knowledge and specialized skills necessary to solve/manage this problem ourselves and, therefore, require that they be possessed by the consultants that we engage (list specific knowledge and skills below):

1.

2.

3.

4.

5.

6.

7.

8.

Checklist II.4
Consulting competence

---

4 3 2 1   1. **Analysis and diagnosis**: Our consultant must be willing and able to select, collect, sort and analyse information from relevant sources related to our problem situation, including an ability to identify and distinguish between the symptoms and root causes of a problem.

4 3 2 1 2. **Strategic planning**: Our consultant must be willing and able to help the key members of our organization to formulate, agree on and commit to a 'desired state' and to identify and select from alternative strategies for reaching that state.

4 3 2 1 3. **Change management**: Our consultant must be willing and able to help us to effectively plan for, implement, manage and monitor any changes inherent in resolving our problem situation, including demonstrating a high degree of skill in effectively managing the dynamics inherent in adoption of and resistance to change at the individual, group and organizational levels.

4 3 2 1 4. **Evaluation**: Our consultant must be willing and able to develop and implement valid strategies for identifying and evaluating the intended and unintended results of the consulting services provided.

Checklist II.5
Interpersonal competence

4 3 2 1 1. **Confrontation skills**: Our consultant must be willing and able to openly surface and confront behaviours and conditions contributing to our problem situation even when doing so may drastically increase the discomfort of influential organizational members who would prefer to avoid such 'sensitive' issues.

4 3 2 1 2. **Risk-taking skills**: Our consultant must be willing and able to take 'acceptable risks', including working outside of his/her personal comfort zone and actively modelling appropriate risk-taking behaviours.

4 3 2 1 3. **Collaboration**: Our consultant must be willing and able to cooperate and collaborate effectively with the managers, leaders and members of our organization; s/he must also be able to distinguish between being collaborative and being compliant and will not compromise his/her professional integrity to avoid necessary but unpleasant reactions or confrontations.

4 3 2 1 4. **Conflict management**: Our consultant must hold an appropriately positive view of conflicts and be willing and able to

use them as an opportunity for synergistic problem-solving and growth at the individual and group level; s/he must be aware of and actively seek to avoid inappropriate and ineffective compromise or win–lose solutions.

4 3 2 1   4.   **Relationship building**: Our consultant must be willing and able to establish and maintain trusting relationships with the managers and members of our organization; s/he must be credible and able to earn the trust of others easily and relatively quickly.

Checklist II.6
Interpersonal competence

Fill in the specific experience that you require of your consultant in each of the three following areas:

1.   Our consultant must have experience with dealing effectively with the following types of problem:

2.   Our consultant must have experience working at the following organizational levels:

3.   Our consultant must have experience working with the following types of organizations and industries:

Checklist II.7
Personal characteristics

4 3 2 1   1.   **Personal characteristics:** Our consultant must be able to describe and manage his/her own strengths and weaknesses in a balanced manner, that is, in a way that is neither too arrogant and aloof nor too humble and wishy-washy.

4 3 2 1   2. **Results-oriented**: Our consultant must clearly demonstrate a need to set and achieve both short- and long-term goals for his/her activities; s/he must be willing and able to set and be motivated to achieve clear, concise mileposts and clearly defined overall project goals.

4 3 2 1   3. **Ability to manage personal needs**: Our consultant must be well aware of his/her own needs and be willing and able to appropriately manage these needs as s/he works within our organization; s/he must be especially aware of and able to manage his/her personal needs for power and influence and for close personal contact.

4 3 2 1   4. **Ability to manage personal style preferences**: Our consultant must have the 'it' that we are looking for (use the space below to describe what 'it' is):

4 3 2 1   5. **Core values**: The three most important core values that our consultant must possess in order to work effectively within our organization in this problem situation are the following:

III

CHOOSING THE BEST CONSULTANT FOR THE JOB

❖

5

LOCATING PROSPECTIVE CONSULTANTS

❖

Now that you've developed a selection criteria that defines the type and quality of consultant that you require, it's time to begin narrowing down the field to four to five 'short-listed' consultant candidates. There are five primary methods by which you can identify consultant candidates for your short list. Listed in reverse order of value, they are:

1. brochures distributed by a consultant or consulting firm,
2. direct selling by a consultant or consulting firm,
3. contacts made at professional conferences,
4. capability presentations facilitated by the consulting firm, and
5. referrals by a credible third party.

CONTACT THROUGH BROCHURES

Most brochures mailed out by consulting firms end up in the circular file under the secretary's desk. The reasons for this are twofold. First, most managers do not have time to read the daily avalanche of brochures they receive. Second, most managers have learned from experience that it is virtually impossible to distinguish a competent, qualified consultant from a huckster on the basis of a brochure. Actually, the circular file is probably the best place for the majority of brochures from consulting firms because most are of little real value and many are consciously misleading.

Case in point

One of the most impressive brochures that we have ever seen from a consulting firm was consciously designed to make the firm look larger, more prestigious and more experienced than it actually is. Although the firm consists of a single consultant and a part-time secretary, it took a lesson from the Remington Steele television series and chose a name along the lines of 'Smith, Rembrandt and Associates, Management Consultants', of whom only Smith exists – Rembrandt is a fictitious name and there are no formal associates.

On the back of the brochure is an impressive list of fifteen to twenty well-known organizations that have supposedly 'benefited' from the consulting firm's services, but the brochure fails to tell you *how* they have benefited, that is, what, specifically, the consultant did for these firms. Nor does the brochure tell you whom to contact within these organizations in order to gain a more specific reference. Not only is this list worthless as a measure of a consultant's experience; it is also clearly misleading. For example, although Smith did, in fact, do work for one of the prestigious firms listed, her involvement was done under the close supervision of a senior consultant from another consulting firm and consisted of running a one-week training programme for first line supervisors. There is a great difference between 'I consulted with Fortune 500' and 'I helped run a one-week course for supervisors at Fortune 500'.

Of course, even the worst brochures are not without value. If you read them properly, they will tell you more about the consulting firm than was ever intended. For example, some are so focused on selling you a specific product or service that they forget the simple fact that every organization is unique. In fact, the most reliable criteria for judging between brochures to cast in the waste basket and those to keep for future reference is found in one simple question: 'What is the brochure trying to sell me?' If it is trying to convince you to buy a specific service, product, course, method, or whatever, throw it away. If it is trying to convince you to arrange an initial exploratory meeting with a representative of the consulting firm, it might be worth considering further. The brochures that tend to attract our positive attention are those that clearly indicate the consulting firm's willingness and ability to listen and adapt to the needs of their client organizations. Although such brochures may list some of the organizations with which the consultant has worked, the list will be relatively short, intended only to give the reader a 'feel' for the firm's credibility.

DIRECT SELLING BY CONSULTANTS

Sales calls by consultants seeking to interest you in their products or services can provide you with an excellent opportunity to judge their consulting philosophy, competence, experience, and so on. Unfortunately, it can also consume an inordinate amount of your time and energy, especially if you are too polite to say, 'Look, you're wasting your time and mine – please go away NOW!' Consultants who attempt to sell their services directly to potential clients will usually reveal their true consulting style during the first ten minutes. Some are most interested in impressing you and use the meeting to tell you about who they know, where they have been and what they have done to help other client organizations. The consultants worth considering are those who clearly demonstrate, from the beginning, that they are sincerely interested in you and your situation and who focus the meeting by asking questions and listening to your answers.

Case in point

The Managing Director of a medium sized chain of retail stores keeps a file of what she considers 'interesting' brochures from consulting firms, sorted by the type of services that the firm offers. When she believes that she needs external help with a given problem she simply takes out the appropriate file of brochures and thumbs through them to find the one(s) that seem most interesting. Recently she had been hearing a lot about 'visioning', 'futuring', and similar approaches to proactively managing the organization's future. She didn't know much about what such terms involved, so she went through her brochures and found one that, in addition to appearing very professional, touted the consulting firm's 'Strategic Planning for the New Millennium'. Because the words 'visioning' and 'future' appeared several times in the brochure, she decided that it might be valuable to contact the consulting firm to find out more about the concept of 'visioning' and its possible value to her organization.

A week after contacting the consulting firm she was visited by one of the firm's 'Senior Consultants' who, incidentally, appeared to be exceptionally young for such a title. The consultant began well; 'I understand you are interested in our Strategic Planning for the New Millennium programme'. The MD's positive nod was all the assurance the consultant needed to launch into a 35-minute presentation of his 'unique', 'powerful', 'dynamic' programme. The exceptionally few questions that he asked were clearly calculated to build the foundation for the next stage of his presentation. For example, when it was time to demonstrate how his programme 'helped busy executives to coordinate their planning calendars', the consultant asked, 'Do you ever have difficulty coordinating the planning calendars of your executives?' (Show us a senior executive that doesn't have this problem and we'll show you a one-person company!)

CONTACT ESTABLISHED AT PROFESSIONAL CONFERENCES

Professional conferences can provide an excellent opportunity for you to make contact with potential consultants if you use them properly. If used improperly, they will provide you with a tonne of worthless brochures, a pile of embossed business cards and a severe headache from listening to too many people trying to convince you that they are the best at whatever it is that they do. Many professional conferences provide exhibition areas where consultants can display themselves, their products and services, but the most interesting consultant candidates are seldom found there. They will be sitting beside you during the presentations wearing a participants' name tag. That is, the consultants of most value to you will be focusing their attention on increasing their knowledge, information and skill, not selling themselves or their firm to other participants. If a consultant is spending more time telling and selling than listening and learning, s/he is probably not the person you need!

You should also be aware that only relatively large consulting firms set up display booths and hospitality suites at such events. As a result, you are unlikely to find the highly effective independent consultant or two to three person consulting firm behind a booth in the exhibitor's area. If you do visit the exhibition area, we strongly recommend that you *do not* waste your time, and endanger your back, by scurrying around stuffing as many brochures as possible into plastic exhibition bags. You will benefit far more by seeking out and talking one-to-one with consultants than from reading their marketing materials after the conference.

CONSULTANT CAPABILITY PRESENTATIONS

One of the best, most proactive and seldomly used methods for gaining insight into the true capabilities of a consultant or consulting firm is to invite them into your firm for a two to three hour 'capability presentation'. The primary goal of such presentations is to familiarize you and other key members of your organization with the strengths, areas of speciality, approaches, and so on, of potentially usable consulting firms. This will enable you to build a 'pool' of a limited number of consultants and/or consulting firms who you would feel comfortable contacting when and if you have a specific type of problem. Therefore, they should be arranged at a time when you are *not* in immediate need of consulting assistance.

The consultants or consulting firms participating in the capability presentation should be given only minimal instructions and guidance. In addition to relevant time constraints and logistical details, they should be told that they are expected to provide you and your management with a clear picture of their unique strengths, areas of speciality, approach, and so on. How the consultants design and facilitate their presentation will provide you with invaluable data about the firm itself. For example:

○　　The content of their presentation will tell you whether they are Training Consultants, Expert Consultants, Process Consultants – or something else (masquerading as a consultant).

○　　The amount of time they spend telling and selling versus asking and listening will tell you if they are 'hammer salesmen' or consultants.

○　　The proportion of the allotted time they focus on themselves compared to the amount of time they focus on you, your organization and the unique problem(s) that you face will tell you how hungry they are and whose needs they are likely to prioritize; yours or their own.

○　　How they handle 'unexpected' events during their presentation will tell you a great deal about their flexibility. In fact we suggest that you consciously throw prospective consultants a curve or two, for example, informing them that they have 10 minutes more or less time than originally agreed upon, having more people in attendance than originally stated, or whatever.

○　　How they respond to your questions and concerns will provide insight into their honesty, openness and willingness to confront.

○　　The degree to which you or other key members of your organization learned something of practical value as a direct result of their presentation will provide you with an indication of the consultants' willingness and ability to transfer their skills and knowledge to the members of your organization.

Case in point

One of our client organizations has a policy of sponsoring a 'capability presentation' every month. All members of the organization's senior management team are expected to attend these presentations which are usually scheduled for two hours and are followed by a relatively informal lunch to which the presenters are invited. After lunch the senior management team meets for one hour to discuss the presentation, focusing on such questions as:

1.　　What can we learn from what was presented?
2.　　To what degree does the consultant or consulting firm fit our culture, values, and so on?
3.　　To what degree would we be interested in engaging this consultant or consulting firm in the future? Why? Why not?
4.　　For what types of problems would we engage this consultant or consulting firm? Why?
5.　　If we did engage this consultant or consulting firm, what types of problems might we expect and how could these problems best be avoided/managed?

The answers to the above questions are kept in a database that is readily accessible when the organization finds itself in need of external assistance.

CONTACT THROUGH REFERRALS

Many of the most skilled, effective consultants have a strong aversion to direct, face-to-face marketing and cold-call selling. As a result, they do not market themselves at all. Others are so involved with current consulting assignments that they have little time left over to actively market themselves to new clients. Still others have no need to market themselves because they are already heavily booked for one to two years into the future. How do such consultants get their assignments? Almost all rely heavily on word-of-mouth referrals from satisfied clients to attract new clients. Such referrals are, beyond a doubt, the best way for capable, professional consultants and clients with a specific problem to find each other. Unfortunately, unless you are in contact with someone who has used and is pleased with a specific consultant, you may never find out that s/he exists. The best way to remedy this situation is for you to personally develop, and/or get involved in, a network of senior managers who have had recent experience with a wide variety of consultants.

If you are relying on references as the basis of judging the quality of a consultant candidate, make sure that the person providing the reference is credible and is not acting in their own personal interest. We know of one senior executive whose private opinion of a specific big name consulting firm was that they 'ripped us off'. Yet, when he was approached by a colleague who was considering using the same consulting firm and asked for a reference, he gave the consulting firm a glowing reference. Why? For the simple reason that he had paid over £2,000,000 for the services of this consulting firm and was not about to admit to a respected colleague that that amount of money had been virtually wasted.

TWO ADDITIONAL POINTS TO CONSIDER

Before moving on to our suggestions for how to best manage the process of interviewing potential consultants, there are two peripheral questions that you should consider: (1) 'What's in a name?', and (2) 'If the consultant is so good, why is s/he available?'

WHAT'S IN A NAME?

We have come to the conclusion that a large advertising budget can, in fact, compensate for a low level of competence and professionalism. How else can one explain the fact that many executives, such as the two in the previous case, choose their consultants based solely on the consulting firm's size, prestigious name, astronomical fees, and so on, with little investigation into the firm's true capabilities and/or track record.

Case in point

The Director of a national public agency decided it was time to 'take the temperature' of his organization. Based on their billboards, adverts and PR, he 'knew' that XYZ Consulting, Inc. was the largest, most prestigious consulting firm in his area and assumed that they were the most competent. He contacted XYZ and shortly thereafter was visited by one of their 'Senior Consulting Partners' who presented an extremely professional, competent and confident image. As a result, the Director engaged XYZ to conduct a complete assessment of his organization's strengths and weaknesses. The assessment process took approximately a month. During that time the Senior Consulting Partner was noticeably absent. The actual assessment was conducted by a staff of 'Junior Consultants', most of whom appeared to be newly-minted MBA graduates with little or no real-world experience.

After the assessment the Senior Consulting Partner arranged for a meeting with the Director to 'deliver the results of the assessment'. The Director was shocked to find that what he received from the consultant was not a presentation but four binders with statistical 'assessment findings' and one binder with recommendations. He was even more shocked when he discovered that he was already well aware of 95 per cent of the assessment 'findings'. What infuriated him most, however, was that the vast majority of the recommendations fell into one or more of the following five categories:

O   measures that had already been implemented but had been missed by the consultants when they conducted their 'comprehensive' assessment;

O   potential actions that had already been considered by the organization's management and rejected for valid reasons;

O   recommendations that seemed to have no logical relationship to the assessment data provided or to the problems the consultants were engaged to investigate;

O   measures that were unintelligible; and/or

O   measures that were extremely naive, theoretical or unrealistic, in other words, measures which were typical of the textbook solutions that newly-minted MBA's would develop for textbook

> cases. (As one senior manager commented, 'Most of these recommendations seem to have come out of a textbook – what do they have to do with us?')

The Director in the above case made the mistake of putting all of his faith in the prestigious name of the consulting firm and the impressive Senior Consulting Partner who represented it. Because he was unaware of the 'bait and switch' tactic used by many large consulting firms, he did not ask such vital questions as: 'Who will be doing the work involved in this contract?'; 'If someone other than you will be involved, what are their qualifications?'; and so on.

The situation that we describe in the preceding paragraphs has become so rampant that many professional consultants have developed thriving businesses serving what they not-so-jokingly call the 'McKinsey aftermarket'. Although the name McKinsey can, and probably should be replaced by the name of any one of five to ten other large, well known consulting firms, the fact is that many client organizations require immediate and intensive consulting assistance to help them repair the often considerable damage caused by the well known consulting firm that they initially engaged. In fact, as this book is going to press several large, well known consulting firms are being sued by former clients for non-delivery of promised results. Because most of these cases are still pending, we cannot reveal names. However, many of these law suits have arisen because the consulting firm appears to have limited their responsibility to the assessment of the problem situation and delivery of a set of recommendations. Their clients, on the other hand, expected those recommendations to be realistic, relevant and practical. That is, they may not have expected consultant help with implementation, but they expected the recommendations to be implementable.

We strongly recommend that, no matter how prestigious the consulting firm might be, you ask them, 'Have any of your recent clients been disappointed in the services provided by your firm?'. If so, 'Why were they disappointed?', 'What did your firm do about it?', 'What would you have done differently?', and, most importantly, 'What are you going to do to ensure that we are satisfied with the services that you deliver to us?' You might also consider asking, 'What has your consulting firm done in the last five years to uphold its reputation' and 'What have you, personally, done to keep your skills and knowledge up to date?'

We also suggest that you are brutally honest with yourself regarding the criteria that you use to select a consulting firm. Are you more interested in what the consultant can do for you and your organization or is your primary goal to impress your peers, colleagues and professional associates by being able to tell them that we have engaged a prestigious consultant or consulting firm?

CONSULTANT AVAILABILITY

After fifty years of combined consulting experience we have to admit that what frustrates us most about our clients is the same as that which our personal doctors must find frustrating in us.

Case in point

Both of the authors of this book have chosen doctors with reputations as being among the best general practitioners available in their geographical area. That means that both of our doctors are in high demand. This, in turn, means that it is extremely difficult to book an appointment at short notice; a fact which we both accept – in theory. After all, who would trust a doctor who had so few patients that s/he could regularly accommodate patients on short notice? However, in practice, when we, personally, need medical attention, we tend to expect our doctors to make an immediate hole in their busy schedules to accommodate our needs.

To make matters worse, we find that both of us do the same thing to our doctors that we complain about in our clients. For example, one of us began experiencing a bit of pain in his side recently. Because he has a very busy consulting schedule he tried to ignore the pain. After three weeks the pain had become more severe and was interfering with his sleep so he began taking an over-the-counter pain remedy with a mild sleep enhancer. By the end of two months the pain had become so severe that he was 'forced' to call his doctor's receptionist and say, 'I have a very serious problem and I need to see the doctor as quickly as possible'.

There are several parallels between the above case and what happens between clients and consultants. Most executives (1) want the best consulting help available, (2) usually wait until their problem is critical before seeking the help that they need, and (3) expect the best consultant to be immediately available.

Our advice for how best to manage such situations in the future is taken directly from the two behaviours that our doctors have requested of us: (1) 'Please make sure that you contact me when you first notice a problem so that we can arrange for a mutually convenient time to take a look before things get serious.' And (2) 'I recommend regularly scheduled check-ups to ensure that we spot problems that you are too busy to notice.' We recommend that you establish an ongoing relationship with a consultant that you trust and use him/her to help you to maintain a proactive perspective on the current and evolving strengths and weaknesses of your organization. We also suggest that you contact your consultant when you begin noticing problems instead of waiting until they become serious.

6

INTERVIEWING PROSPECTIVE CONSULTANTS

❖

Once you have narrowed down the field of prospective consultants to a short list of between four to five likely candidates, your next step is to call each of them in for a selection interview. The goal of this chapter is to provide you with a set of practical tools and concepts aimed at maximizing your chances of selecting the best consultant from among your short-listed candidates. Specifically, we discuss:

○　　　preparing for selection interviews;
○　　　setting the interview climate;
○　　　avoiding destructive games;
○　　　culling 'hungry' consultants;
○　　　getting the information that you need from the prospective consultants;
○　　　providing consultant candidates with what they need to know about you and your organization; and
○　　　requiring a post-interview summary from your consultant candidates.

PREPARING FOR SELECTION INTERVIEWS

In most cases, selection interviews should be conducted by a 'selection committee', comprising three to five members of your organization with joint responsibility for the selection of the most qualified consultant candidate. Selection committee members should not be chosen on the basis of their status or position in your organization. Rather, they should be selected solely on the basis of what their involvement will contribute to the selection of the best possible candidate *and/or* to the acceptance of the selected consultant by other key/influential members of your organization. For example, one of the authors was selected for a recent assignment by a committee composed of:

O   the organization's Managing Director;
O   the HR Director, with whom the consultant was expected to work inten-
     sively;
O   the Production Director, whose function was most involved in the change
     effort to be implemented; and
O   two influential middle managers from within the Production Department;
     one of whom was likely to be supportive of the change and the other
     who was likely to resist the change.

Before commencing the interview process, you and your selection committee
should take ample time to prepare your interview strategy, including:

O   Who else needs to be involved in the screening and selection process in
     order to ensure their support of the selection decision?
O   What, specifically, are your goals for the selection interview in terms of
     what you will have learned and/or decided about the candidate at the
     end of the interview?
O   How, specifically, are you going to ensure that you will achieve these
     goals?
O   What specific questions are you going to ask?
O   How must the prospective consultant respond to your questions in order
     to be seen in a positive light? What might s/he do or say that would cause
     you to be concerned about his/her acceptability?
O   Where should the interview be conducted? Why? What are the advan-
     tages and disadvantages of alternative interview venues in terms of help-
     ing or hindering you in reaching a valid decision?
O   What material should your committee have available to help you to
     describe your organization and its current situation to the prospective
     consultants? What is the best way to present this material?
O   What are the worst things that could happen during the selection inter-
     view? How can you reduce the risk of their occurrence or most effectively
     manage them if they do occur?

SETTING THE INTERVIEW CLIMATE

Clients tend to waste a tremendous amount of valuable time during selection
interviews in something they think of as 'climate setting'. While climate setting is
an essential first step in any meeting, talking about the win/loss record of the local
football team or how rotten the weather has been is *not* climate setting. Rather,
such small talk is more likely a stalling tactic designed to give both parties a
chance to sniff the other out before getting to the meat of the meeting.

A more effective way to establish a meaningful interview climate is to begin
with a clarification of mutual goals for the meeting. We suggest that you, as a

prospective client, take the initiative and ask consultant candidates to define their goals for the meeting before presenting your own. Comparing the quality and contents of the candidates' answers will provide valuable insight into how much preparation each has put into the meeting and how well each is able to think on his/her feet. In addition, the presentation of their goals for the meeting may give you clues to how 'hungry' they are for work. For example, if a consultant dodges the question and immediately enters into a presentation of his/her capabilities, you should start looking for a way to end the interview as quickly as possible! If a consultant candidate is seriously interested in meeting your needs as a client, without sacrificing his/her own, s/he should say something like, 'My primary goal for this meeting is to gain a better understanding of your current situation, what you would like to accomplish, and what you think might be an effective way of achieving your goals.' An exceptionally honest consultant may even state, 'One of my goals is to see if we are compatible enough to work together on the problem that you are seeking help with.'

AVOIDING DESTRUCTIVE GAMES

The selection interview is not the place to play power and/or guessing games. It is the time for open and honest communication between you and short-listed consultant candidates. This does not negate the legitimacy of an appropriate marketing strategy on the part of the consultant or a selection strategy on your part. What is essential is that the interests of both parties are served by the strategies used and that these strategies are *transparent* and understood by both parties. One of the most serious mistakes that you can make during a selection interview is to keep your major needs and goals for the consulting project to yourself. A prospective consultant's energy should be devoted to exploring the degree to which his/her skills match your needs; not to trying to unearth your hidden agendas and/or avoiding the risk of 'saying the wrong thing'. Human nature is such that people tend to protect themselves and become less open or self-disclosing when they sense that the other person has a hidden agenda or purpose. If that happens in a selection interview you may discover that the individual that you engaged bears little resemblance to the individual that you interviewed because s/he skilfully hid behind a mask that you found attractive.

CULLING 'HUNGRY' CONSULTANTS

A consultant's goal for the first meeting with a prospective client *should never be* to sell his/her consulting services. Consultants' primary goals for an initial selection interview should be to identify your concerns and to explore the possibility that their skills can help you and/or other members of your organization to effectively deal with those concerns. Any consultant more interested in getting a contract and/or earning fees than in ensuring that s/he can help you to solve your problem(s) in a cost-beneficial way is 'hungry', and hungry consultants are extremely dangerous animals.

There are a number of ways to detect 'hungry' consultants. Some obvious signals include:

○ Consultants who take up the majority of the interview trying to convince you of their credibility by talking about themselves, their consulting firm and their experience are clearly hungry. The same is true of those who waste valuable time telling 'war stories' about all of the marvellous work that they have carried out for other clients.

○ Consultants who continually link your situation to other assignments that they have worked on are usually insecure and/or trying to gain your respect and appreciation – therefore, they are hungry.

○ Consultants who quickly respond to a general definition of your situation by prescribing a specific solution without probing deeper into probable causes or suggesting a more in-depth assessment are typically hungry.

Hungry consultants may not be incompetent, but they may be so anxious about their revenues that they are vulnerable to prioritizing their own needs over the needs of your organization. *It is up to you to ensure that hungry consultants are not allowed to feed off you or your organization.*

GETTING THE INFORMATION THAT YOU NEED FROM THE PROSPECTIVE CONSULTANT

What should you find out about short-listed consultant candidates? The answer to this question is found in the selection criteria established earlier in this book. You and the members of your selection committee should ask questions that will help you to identify each consultant candidate's (a) consulting philosophy, (b) technical competence, (c) competence in basic consulting processes, (d) interpersonal competence and (e) applicable personal characteristics. In addition, we suggest that you explore the following specific questions:

Question 1: Of all that there is to perceive within your organization, what is this consultant most likely to actually see and hear? The possible elements of your organization that a consultant might perceive encompass a large range of dimensions, qualities, attributes and processes. They include your organization's culture, vision and mission, structures, policies and procedures, rules and regulations, financial position, technologies, levels of employee empowerment, and so on. Competent consultants generally use some form of 'diagnostic model' to organize and interpret the myriad of possible organizational elements and dynamics that can be assessed and attended to. The model that the consultant uses will determine what s/he looks for and responds to within your organisation. We recommend that you ask consultant candidates to present and explain the diagnostic model they would use in working with your organization to ensure that they have such a model, that you understand and agree with it and that it is appropriate to your organization and the task at hand.

Question 2: Of all that the consultant perceives, what is likely to register as having diagnostic significance? Several years ago, as the story goes, a group of highly respected consultants from different specialities were presented with the description of a problem situation within an organization and asked what they would do to resolve it. A consultant who specialized in communications skills saw it as a communications problem and recommended a series of communications workshops. A consultant who specialized in goal-setting saw the problem as resulting from unclear goals and objectives and recommended a goal-setting workshop for senior management. A consultant who specialized in employee relations was certain that middle-managers were not sufficiently empowered and recommended a change in the structure to decentralize decision-making downward in the hierarchy.

Whether this story is true or not is debatable. What is not debatable is the dynamic that it portrays. All too often, consultants see what they want to see and, all too often, what they want to see is a problem that is directly related to the services that they are most prepared to offer. One way to discover whether a prospective consultant is in a professional rut is to ask him/her to describe the types of activities s/he has performed over the last couple of years. If it seems that most of these activities are of the same basic type, you might ask what clues s/he looked for in determining what type of intervention was necessary in each of the cases presented. You might also ask what clues would have been necessary to convince him/her that some other type of intervention would have been more appropriate.

Question 3: To what degree is the consultant selling panaceas? Many consultants seem to believe that almost any problem in the vast majority of organizations can be solved by the pre-packaged programme (such as performance management, TQM, customer service, reengineering) that they offer. This 'one size fits all' philosophy tends to be characteristic of inexperienced, naïve, or mass market-oriented consultants. Although such programmes *may* be beneficial in many circumstances, we categorically reject the idea that any programme can be universally applicable. In fact, we believe that an over-dependence on any single change strategy is very likely to decrease rather than increase your organization's long-term effectiveness. If any of your consultant candidates seems to be promoting a 'panacea' solution, you may want to respond as did one of our clients to a 'hammer salesman': 'I am amazed. In a mere 15 minutes you have been able to identify the primary cause of a major problem that my colleagues and I have been grappling unsuccessfully with for months. Not only that. I have had the extreme good fortune of finding a consultant who is already prepared with a perfect solution to our problem. How do you explain my great good fortune?'

Question 4: Is the consultant aware of and able to manage the differences between consulting under 'crisis' conditions as opposed to consulting under 'steady state' conditions? There is a great deal of difference between consulting under 'crisis' or 'emergency' conditions and consulting under 'healthy' or 'steady state' conditions. If you are in a crisis situation, you should be looking for a consultant who is fast-paced, attentive to both strategic and tactical issues and clearly results-oriented. In addition, s/he should be highly proactive, that is, not waiting to be asked before acting. S/he should focus attention on evident critical factors or events that may not be recognized (or felt) by you or your managers, organization members or stakeholders.

In our experience, this description best fits Technical Experts. They are generally prepared to move in, make rapid diagnoses of the situation, formulate recommendations, and/or take corrective action. In short, they are usually more oriented to the technical issues than to the people issues, and this is often what is needed to survive a crisis. However, many Technical Experts are so task and action oriented that they don't take the time to understand how people feel and behave in crisis conditions and fail to help them to regain the sense of personal control over the situation. In short, the best consultant in a crisis is often a Technical Expert who has a firm foundation in the skills of a Process Consultant.

Steady state conditions require that the consultant practice 'operational consulting', namely, that s/he adopt a more process-oriented, responsive consulting style. Although the consultant should still be problem-focused and results-oriented, s/he should typically allow more time for the members of your organization to personally explore, experiment with and discover their own needs as well as those of your organization. More importantly, s/he may consciously reduce the speed of the change process to ensure that you and the members of your organization learn from the experience.

Not all consultants recognize the difference between crisis consulting and steady state consulting. Many are so oriented to working under 'steady state' conditions that they neither acknowledge nor adjust to crisis conditions. Others are so addicted to the adrenaline rush of surviving a crisis that they become quickly bored in steady state conditions and may go so far as planting the seeds of new crises just to keep things exciting. The best way to determine whether consultant candidates understand and are capable of managing the difference between crisis and steady state consulting is to ask them to provide concrete examples of how they have dealt with both types of situations. As they make their presentations, actively probe what they see as the differences between the two types of situations from a consulting and change management perspective.

Question 5: To what degree does the consultant balance task- and process-related interventions? Many consultants prioritize the resolution of 'softer', more process-related issues such as congenial work relationships, employee satisfaction, empowerment and teamwork, while undervaluing or ignoring the importance of 'harder', more task related issues such as structure, goals and strategy. Such consultants are usually quick to justify their priorities with the (convenient) belief that teamwork, employee satisfaction, empowerment, and so on, are prerequisites to the development of effective organizational structures, goals and strategies. Other consultants prioritize the resolution of harder, more task-related issues. Their argument is that relationship issues can only be resolved within the framework of appropriate organization structures, clear goals and appropriate strategies.

Which of the two polar (chicken and egg) positions is correct? In our view, *neither!* We categorically disagree with anyone who states that the management of softer issues is a prerequisite to effective performance in the harder areas or vice versa. Any consultant who consistently prioritizes one focus over the other is clearly demonstrating his/her weakness as a consultant. Consultants who continually prioritize the soft, relationship side of organizations are often unaware of the simple fact that most organizations exist to produce specific outputs, not make their employees happy. They seem blissfully unaware of the number of organizations in which so much attention was devoted to making people happy that the organization failed. On the other hand, consultants who always prioritize the hard side are often those who feel extremely uncomfortable with and/or threatened by expressions of emotions or intense feelings between individuals and groups (unless it is on the football pitch) and, as a result, do everything in their power to avoid having to face up to serious relationship issues as part of their consulting responsibility. Such consultants often seem to forget that organizations are composed of people, and people are seldom rational and objective in their reactions to things that they perceive as threats. They often fail to appreciate the emotional effects that a significant organizational change can have upon the people within an organization. Nor do they appreciate the simple fact that people experiencing significant emotional stress are likely to react in a number of predictably unpredictable ways, most of which will be detrimental to the organization and to the change effort.

At a minimum consultants who consistently emphasize either process *or* task issues are misguided and, therefore, likely to misguide you and the members of your organization. Both task and process issues are present in all situations and both must typically be addressed, usually simultaneously. For example, it is not really that difficult to develop a strategic plan that is technically correct in all ways – most MBA students can knock out such a plan in a few hours. Nor is it difficult to get a group of senior executives into a heated discussion about the relative merits of any given strategic alternative. What *is* difficult, however, is getting a group of senior executives to synergistically use their different perceptions and opinions to create a strategic plan to which they are all fully committed *as a team*.

The problem with attempting to balance the focus on task and process issues is that the centre of balance (fulcrum) is likely to shift continuously throughout most change efforts. For example, the change effort may begin with a situation that requires an almost even balance between process and task issues, such as ensuring an open and creative group climate while the management team explores different strategic options. That situation may suddenly change to one that requires an almost total emphasis on a process issue; for example, a major interpersonal conflict breaking out between the Production and Marketing Directors. Then, just as suddenly, the situation shifts again to one that requires an almost total emphasis on the harder side, such as, analysing and evaluating the economic effects of two different strategic options. A truly effective consultant is well aware of and able to manage his/her preference for dealing with process- or task-related issues. More importantly, s/he is both willing and able to shift priorities based on the demands of the situation. That is, s/he is equally effective at dealing with task related issues as with relationship related issues, despite the fact that s/he may personally feel more comfortable dealing with one or the other.

It relatively easy to determine if consultant candidates have a preference for process- or task-related issues. Simply ask them to describe their last four or five consulting assignments in terms of 'what, specifically, did you do?' If they immediately begin – and continue – telling you about things like building teams, improving communication, increasing empowerment, and so on, you probably have a process fanatic on your hands. If they focus mostly on things like creating new structures, setting goals, increasing productivity, and so on, you may have a task fanatic to deal with. The individual that you are looking for will clearly demonstrate that they are (1) aware of their personal preference for either task or process issues, but (2) are fully capable of shifting between the two types of issues as the situation requires.

Question 6: To what extent is the consultant likely to accept input from yourself and other key members of your organization? Input to a consultant may consist of feedback about his/her behaviours, direction, methods, or specific actions. It may also be in the form of specific suggestions for alternative approaches to the consulting tasks. Even if a consultant does not agree with the input s/he receives, s/he must clearly demonstrate a willingness to carefully consider input from others. Individuals who place no value on the ideas and opinions of others are not consultants; they are demagogues who should be summarily knocked off their pedestals!

Question 7: Is the consultant able and willing to reveal his/her own personal confusion and uncertainty? No consultant can be totally certain about everything all the time. In fact, confusion may be an advantage. Confucius said, 'To be confused and uncertain is to be open to learning.' Some consultants seem to feel that it is necessary to appear to be in full control, continuously demonstrating that they know *precisely* what should be done, why, how, when, and by whom, in every conceivable situation. This can be extremely disconcerting, especially if you or members of your organization are feeling the opposite. Consultants who have mastered the appearance of stoicism and refrain from disclosing their confusion or uncertainty in any way may do this for many different reasons. They may fear that uncertainty would cause them to appear to be incompetent or foolish. Or, they may believe it is important to appear to be imperturbable or decisive to specific members of your organization. In the latter case, there may be some justification. If the consultant appears confused, uncertain and indecisive during an emergency, organizational members may become contaminated by the consultant's anxieties.

Some consultants are very effective in describing and using their confusion and uncertainty to the benefit of their client organization and its members. The consultant's confusion can model the fact that uncertainty is not only a natural state when confronting an unprecedented situation, but that it can also lead to an effective collaborative problem-solving effort: 'I'm a bit confused; can you help me?' Even though organizational members may want to rely upon a 'heroic' consultant to pull them through a chaotic situation, they will usually benefit more when they discover that even the consultant does not have a magical solution. In such cases, the consultant's greatest contribution can be to increase members' self-confidence in times of future uncertainty by guiding them through an effective problem-solving process which enables them to discover their own capabilities to deal effectively with uncertainty .

Question 8: Does the consultant have the courage to point out that 'the emperor is not wearing any clothes'? Almost every organization has unsayable issues, sacred cows, unchallengeable traditions, and so on. Clearly, considerable courage may be required for organizational members to take the risk of testing the validity of their negative fantasies about the consequences of raising such issues. That is why consultants often find themselves in the position of doing and saying things that the members of the organization perceive as extremely risky. In effect, the consultant can take it upon him/herself to serve as a model for appropriate risk-taking behaviour in the organization. During selection interviews, you might want to ask how the consultant has dealt with sensitive issues in the past. Does s/he appear to be the type of consultant who is both willing and able to appropriately confront sensitive issues, including 'public secrets'? Or, is s/he the type of consultant who is likely to play it safe, colluding with the members of your organization to sweep sensitive issues under the carpet?

PROVIDING CONSULTANT CANDIDATES WITH WHAT THEY NEED TO KNOW

It is not easy to determine in advance how much information you should divulge to a consultant who, at this stage, is still under consideration. If you divulge too much you may find that you have told (rejected) consultants more about your business than you really want them (or your competitors) to know. On the other hand, if you divulge too little you deny the consultant an opportunity to gain essential insights into your organization and its needs. As a result, the consultant will be less able to accurately determine if s/he can, or even wants to, be of assistance.

Some of the things that are important for your consultant candidates to know include:

○   What is the primary problem for which you are considering engaging a consultant?

○   How, specifically, is this problem affecting your organization and its intended outputs?

○   How important is this problem? To whom is it most important?

○   What are the probable consequences of not addressing or dealing with it?

○   What personal stake do you or other key members of your organization have in the problem?

○   What are your expectations regarding the consultant and his/her role in dealing with the problem?

○   What, if anything, has already been done in an effort to deal with the problem? What were the results?

○   What previous experiences have you and your organization had with consultants? What types of consultants have been used? What worked well and what worked less well? What contributed to the positive or negative results obtained?

○   What other major events, circumstances or activities are currently taking place in your organization and how might these affect: (1) your own personal commitment to this consulting effort, (2) the commitment of others who would/should be involved in this consulting effort, (3) the availability of resources for this consulting effort, and/or (4) the results of this effort?

○   How much support are you and other influential organizational members willing to personally commit to the consulting effort?

○   How much time, energy, resources and budget is your organization willing to invest in order to ensure that the problem is dealt with effectively.

○   When, honestly, do you expect this consulting effort to begin and what are your expected deadlines for its completion?

○   What are the criteria for selecting a consultant for this assignment?

○   When and how will the formal selection be made?

If a prospective consultant does not ask for the above information, s/he may be naïve, anxious or hungry. In any event, tell him/her anyway, no later than 30 minutes before the scheduled end of the interview. Take careful note of his/her reactions to this information. If s/he doesn't recognize it as significant and asks few follow-up questions, you probably have an incompetent or hungry consultant on your hands. Further, pay attention to the particular topics about which the consultant asks follow-up questions. These may reflect his/her areas of strength and personal interests. Where s/he does not ask, s/he may be avoiding areas of weakness.

REQUIRING A POST-INTERVIEW SUMMARY FROM YOUR CONSULTANT CANDIDATES

While the selection interview can reveal a great deal about a prospective consultant, an extremely effective method for gaining even more data is to request each consultant candidate to submit a summary report of the selection interview. If the consultant is truly competent his/her summary will include:

O   A set of proposed goals for the consulting assignment which clearly reflect your primary concerns and intentions, but need not necessarily agree with them entirely.

O   His/her perceptions of the major issues/problems raised during the interview, including a summary of what s/he has learned about your organization's strengths and weaknesses relevant to those issues/problems.

O   A summary of additional information that s/he would need for clarity before submitting a formal proposal, including a preliminary plan for gathering additional data related to the nature of the problem and its ultimate solution.

O   A list of references which includes the names of organizations in which s/he has worked with related problems, the nature of the work done, the names of key individuals in those organizations that can be contacted as references and their telephone numbers.

Any truly professional consultant will take time directly after any meeting with a client to thoroughly reflect on what transpired during that meeting. In addition to considering what they, personally and professionally, did well and not so well during the meeting, their reflections will touch on each of the areas described above. As a result, a truly professional consultant should be able to provide you with a comprehensive meeting summary within 24 hours of being interviewed by your selection committee. Any consultant candidates who inform you that they need more than 48 hours to prepare their post-interview summary have not planned their time well and are probably not professional enough to be seriously considered for the assignment. However, you might ask them, 'When had you planned to take the time to do a thorough reflection of our meeting today?'

IF NOBODY QUALIFIES...

Data you gather during the selection interview, together with an evaluation of the prospective consultant's post-interview summary, should enable you and your selection committee to make an informed choice of the consultant who best meets your selection criteria. Once you have thoroughly reviewed all candidates, one of two things may happen. First, you may find that none of the candidates fulfils your criteria. Second, you may find that the consultant that you want is not available. What do you do then?

If none of the consultants interviewed meets your predefined needs and preferences, you will have to make another type of choice. If your organization is in a crisis situation you may feel that you have to engage a less than fully acceptable consultant. If you choose this alternative, be careful! A consultant who is available and willing, but who lacks the necessary competence and experience may be far worse than no consultant at all. It may be well worth investing additional time to extend your search until you find an acceptable candidate.

If the consultant you choose is not available in the near future, you also have alternatives. You can accept the best available consultant as a stop-gap measure while you wait for the consultant you want to become available or you can delay the change effort until the consultant that you want is available. Either way, you are likely to pay a price. If you begin the effort with a less than competent consultant, they may do more damage than good during the interim period. If you decide to wait, the situation itself may deteriorate to the point that even a competent consultant may be of little assistance. What's the solution? *Don't wait until the last minute to seek help!*

7

EVALUATING CONSULTANT PROPOSALS AND CONTRACTS

❖

Hopefully at the conclusion of the last of your selection interviews you have reduced your short list to two or three qualified consultant candidates. Your next task is to request each of the survivors to submit a formal proposal for how they would perform the work inherent in the assignment for which they are being considered. Again, we suggest that you do not provide your candidates with guidelines for the contents of their proposal or how it should be structured, even if they ask.

A consulting proposal and a consulting contract are, and should be, very similar documents. The major difference between them is the purpose for which the two documents are written. A consulting proposal is written to enable you and your selection committee to further review and evaluate a consultant candidate's appropriateness for the assignment for which s/he is being considered. As such, it should provide a basis for comparing one consultant's understanding, approach, strategy and fees against those of the remaining consultants on your short list. A consulting contract is a legal document which should provide a detailed summary of the specific agreements that you and the selected consultant have negotiated relative to the assignment.

WHAT SHOULD A CONSULTING PROPOSAL CONTAIN?

Well written consultant proposals typically include the following sections:

○ a situation description;
○ overall project goals;
○ a problem analysis strategy;
○ a project plan;
○ roles and responsibilities;

101

O   a strategy for evaluating ongoing and final project results; and
O   a summary of anticipated consulting fees and charges.

A SITUATION DESCRIPTION

The consultant's understanding of your current situation should serve as the base from which s/he has formulated all other content in the proposal. Therefore, early in the proposal, the consultant should present a summary which will reveal the extent to which s/he has heard, understood and appreciated issues raised in the interview. This summary should include:

O   a description of the problem(s) which s/he is being asked to help resolve, including a discussion of such key points as why the problem is important, to whom it is important, and so on;
O   a description of how the problem is impacting on relevant individual, group and/or organizational outputs;
O   a discussion of what the consultant knows about the problem, its causes, and impacts, including a discussion of forces currently acting to support and/or restrain changes in the current situation;
O   a discussion of what the consultant does not know about the problem, its causes and impacts including his/her strategy for dealing with the current lack of information;
O   a discussion of measures that you have already taken in an attempt to deal with the problem situation, including the results of those measures and their impact upon the consultant's recommended approach; and
O   any other measures that you, the client, have considered, including a discussion of why these measures have not been implemented.

Competent consultants will not restrict their description of the current situation to a mere repetition of the data that you presented during your initial meeting. They will also provide a specific description of the situation as they, personally, perceive it, including possible incongruencies or holes in the picture that you have presented. Finally, they will point out that their description of the current situation is 'provisional' because they have not as yet had an opportunity to verify your perceptions with other organizational members and/or significant stakeholders.

OVERALL PROJECT GOALS

The proposal should contain a clear description of how you, the client, want the situation to be at the conclusion of the consulting activity, stated in the form of concise, measurable goals. Competent consultants may also provide what they perceive as alternative, more appropriate goals for the project. However, any differences between their recommended goals and your initial goals should be fully justified in terms of how the change will benefit you and your organization. Any goals presented in the proposal should be stated in the form of concrete, observable, measurable targets against which the actual end results of the project will be evaluated.

PROBLEM ANALYSIS STRATEGY

Regardless of the type of consultant you are seeking, his/her first step should be to ensure that s/he has a clear and impartial view of your problem, its impacts and its root causes. Any consultant who does not recommend that the project begin with a thorough assessment of your problem situation is likely to be either too naïve or too hungry to be granted the assignment. The consultant's strategy for analysing your problem situation should include a clarification of:

O   the types of data the consultant will require in order to more fully understand the problem situation;

O   what s/he considers to be the best sources of that data;

O   the methods s/he will use to gather information from these sources, including a discussion of why these methods are preferable to other alternative methods;

O   the degree to which you and/or other members of your organization will be required to be actively involved in the analysis and sorting of information gathered; and

O   how information gathered will be fed back to you and other members of your organization, including the degree to which the consultant will facilitate discussions intended to help you and others to identify and prioritize the key problems.

A PROJECT PLAN

In most cases there will be a clear distinction between project plans submitted by Expert Consultants and those submitted by Process Consultants. If you are seeking an Expert Consultant s/he should be expected to provide you with a very detailed action plan covering each step of the consulting effort, from problem analysis to submission of their final request for payment. Each step in their plan should be clearly linked to the project goals presented at the beginning of their proposal. A calendar of events should also be included to indicate when each step is to begin and when it is expected to be completed.

Process Consultants have two biases that result in them seldom including detailed project plans as part of their proposals. First, they believe that it is impossible to develop a strategy for resolving a problem until that problem has been thoroughly analysed in terms of its strength, its root causes, why it continues to exist, who is 'winning' from its existence, and so on. Second, they do not believe in solving problems 'for' their clients. They prefer, instead, to involve relevant members of their client organization in the problem-solving process. Therefore, rather than include detailed action plans in their proposals, they will typically limit their presentation to a concise description of how you and other key members of your organization will be involved in the analysis of the problem and development of the action plan.

However, regardless of the type of consultant you choose, the plan submitted should be in the form of concise, easily understood steps. Each step should have its own distinct set of measurable objectives that are clearly linked to the overall goals of the project and to all preceding and following steps. Said differently, the objectives for each individual step in the consultant's plan should serve as mileposts for the overall journey to the agreed end results of the project.

ROLES AND RESPONSIBILITIES

Most conflicts between clients and their consultants arise because they have different perceptions of who is responsible for what.

Case in point

One of our colleagues maintains his offices at a large training centre where the lease includes use of a modern training room at no extra charge. Shortly after moving into his offices he was asked to design and facilitate a five-week training course for the managers of a new client company. In his proposal the consultant had specified a set price for the training which 'includes materials, supplies, and the training venue'. In the consultant's mind, the term 'training venue' included the training room, furniture, fixtures and equipment. It did not include 'extras' such as participant lunches during the five-week course.

Throughout the 25 days of the course all 18 programme participants thoroughly enjoyed the training centre's excellent and quite expensive buffet lunches. A week after the course the consultant was contacted by the very upset Training Director of his client organization. The Training Director demanded to know why she had received an invoice for '450 executive lunches' when it was 'clearly stated in the proposal that the consultant would cover the costs of the training venue'. 'But I assumed that lunches were...', began the consultant. 'There is nothing to assume', interrupted the client. 'Either you cover this invoice or forget about working for us in the future.'

Your consultants' proposals should clearly define: (1) your specific responsibilities, as the client, during the entire consulting project, (2) the consultant's specific responsibilities, and (3) the responsibilities of any other involved parties within the organization. This will include, but is not necessarily restricted to, such factors as:

O   Who is responsible for clerical and administrative costs such as copying, typing, and so on.

O   Who is responsible for arranging and paying for venues, meals, lodging and travel.

O   Which members of the consulting firm are to be involved in this project? In what way? When?

O   Which individuals or groups from the client organization are to be involved in this project? In what way? When?

O   How, specifically, are decisions to be made relevant to significant aspects of this project?

O   How much contact is expected to be required between the consultant and the organization's senior executives, individually or as a group?

O   How and when is responsibility for the implementation of recommended actions to be allocated?

O   Who is responsible for evaluating the interim and final results of the project?

In evaluating your consultants' proposals it is important to remember that every task or responsibility that is assigned to the consultant or a member of his/her staff will increase the fees and charges that you incur for the assignment. Although it will usually be less expensive if you rely on your internal staff to carry out some of the tasks, the use of such staff is not without costs. For example, the task of arranging an interview schedule for 25–30 managers and/or employees can be extremely time consuming for the person responsible for contacting all interview subjects, agreeing on suitable interview times, arranging appropriate venues, and so on. If that person is your executive secretary, s/he will be inaccessible to you for several hours, if not a couple of days, while s/he grapples with the logistics of the interview schedule. As a result, although you may save money by doing things internally, the actual costs may be greater than anticipated and than is acceptable.

STRATEGY FOR EVALUATION OF ONGOING AND FINAL PROJECT RESULTS

When should a client and consultant begin discussing the topic of project evaluation? The answer is simple. Evaluation should be discussed at the same time you are negotiating the primary goals and interim objectives of the consulting effort. That means your consulting candidates should dedicate a relatively significant portion of their proposals to such issues as:

O   How, specifically, will achievement of overall project goals be evaluated, when, and by whom, in order to determine the degree to which the project has met the expectations set for it?

○ What specific, measurable mileposts will be used to ensure that the project is on track?
○ How, specifically, will achievement of mileposts be evaluated, when, and by whom?
○ To whom will evaluation results to be reported?
○ How will decisions be made should there be any need to alter the original project plan?

Please note that we consider the evaluation of consulting efforts to be so important that we have devoted a large section of Chapter 8 to the topic.

SUMMARY OF ANTICIPATED CONSULTING FEES AND CHARGES

Proposals submitted by consultant candidates should include a fairly accurate specification of their fees and charges related to each activity described in their action plan. It should also include a clarification of the terms and conditions relevant to how, when and even *if* these fees and charges are to be paid. Consultant fees are typically paid using either a 'time and expense' or a 'fixed price' format. Each of these formats has its unique advantages and disadvantages for both the consultant and the client.

Time and expense formats

Under a time and expense format the consultant is given relative autonomy to deal with a defined problem situation and regularly submits invoices which reflect the amount of consulting time that s/he has expended and any relevant costs or expenses that have been incurred. Such contracts should be used primarily, if not exclusively, for consultants with whom you and your organization are familiar and who have consistently demonstrated a high degree of competence, professionalism, ethics and fiscal integrity. Despite the high degree of trust you place in such consultants, their entrepreneurial efforts must nonetheless be contractually linked to and limited by a specified discretionary budget that the consultant is not allowed to exceed without prior approval.

Consultants working within the time and expense format should also be assigned to a contact person with whom they must negotiate all new agreements not expressly covered in the basic consulting contract. This contact person may be yourself, or a specified individual or group to whom you delegate authority and responsibility for monitoring, evaluating, coordinating, modifying and, if necessary, terminating work being performed by the consultant. The contact person reviews the consultant's invoices, compares the entries against established criteria, conditions and limits, approves or challenges each invoice, and, when satisfied, authorizes payment. If a questionable item is identified, the contact person is responsible for initiating a problem-solving discussion with the consultant.

Fixed price formats

Fixed price formats are straightforward in nature and intent, specifying what, exactly, the consultant is expected to do and what s/he will receive in return. As such, they clearly limit the scope of consultants' activities, the duration of the consulting contract, the costs to your organization and your organization's vulnerability to many forms of consultant 'excesses'. Such contracts can also provide you with an opportunity to test the competence and reputability of an unproved or unknown consultant.

Case in point

The Vice President of Human Resources for a large appliance manufacturer suggested a fixed price consulting contract to one of the authors 'until we get to know you better'. When asked if this was a standard procedure the client replied, 'It has been since last year when we discovered a new consultant padding his expenses and billing us for work that he hadn't done.'

By using a fixed price format you can create a series of natural pauses at which you can review progress and achievements. That is, you can segment the consultation process into specific phases, or on an issue-by-issue basis, with each phase or issue becoming the basis of its own fixed price contract.

The management of fixed price consulting contracts is relatively complex and often awkward for both parties. One of the primary difficulties is that such contracts are based on the assumption that it is possible to anticipate what will transpire during a specific consulting effort. In our experience, this assumption seldom holds true. In fact, we find that 99.9 per cent of all consulting assignments that we are familiar with have required relatively significant changes as they moved from initiation to completion. More importantly, the most drastic changes were usually required relatively early in the assignment as both the consultant and the client learned more about the nature of the problem(s) being dealt with.

Most reputable consultants will inform you at the very beginning of a consulting assignment that the steps and actions included in their proposal may, and probably will, have to be altered as the project progresses. Less reputable consultants will neglect to provide that information because they have become 'upgrade experts'. That is, they consciously quote fees based on unlikely optimal conditions such as full cooperation from everyone involved, no undiscovered issues, no unexpected resistance, no unexpected events, and so on. Once the consultation begins, they 'discover' (read: 'reveal') the need to expand the scope of their assignment. By the time they are done, the assignment and related fees greatly exceed those quoted in rejected proposals from more ethical consultants.

Many experienced, highly reputable consultants accept fixed price format for their initial assignment(s) with a new client with the intention of changing to a time and expense contract once they have gained that client's trust. This strategy may be appropriate when the initial assignment is one that lends itself to a fixed price format. However, when predictable problems begin to emerge that make fee adjustments necessary, the consultant can be perceived either as an amateur who does not understand his/her profession, as a charlatan who is trying to exploit a naïve and trusting client system, or as an incompetent who could not control the situation. Such reactions only decrease a client's faith in the consultant and, as a result, increase the probability that s/he will hold consultants to fixed price agreements in the future.

CONTRACT ADJUSTMENT AND CANCELLATION

The purpose of a consulting contract is to specify and formalize the parameters and limitations of the working agreement between you and the consultant selected for the assignment. This implies that the consulting contract can be interpreted as a binding legal document should either party fail to honour their part of the agreement. The simple fact that a consulting contract is intended to be a legally binding document can lead to a number of complex problems for you and your consultant. For example, it is extremely common that consulting contracts must be adjusted during the consulting project for a number of valid reasons, including:

O   Either you or your consultant has violated or is unable to honour one or more of the essential terms of the contract.

O   Conditions under which the contract was written have changed; for example, a downturn in the economy has caused a reprioritization of your organization's goals and/or the utilization of its scarce resources.

O   You and/or your consultant find it difficult to develop the type of client-consultant relationship needed to continue the effort effectively.

O   Further analysis of the initial issues specified in the contract led to the identification of other, higher priority problems or improvement opportunities which are more suitable to another consultant or consultant type.

O   Your consultant is physically unable to continue the assignment.

O   The person who negotiated and signed the consulting agreement for your organization is replaced by another person who is not supportive of the original consultant or of the consulting project as defined in the contract.

All of the above are valid reasons to reappraise, modify and/or cancel a consulting contract. In the case of a conscious violation of contract terms, the solution is relatively straightforward *if* the terms of the contract were clearly defined and agreed when it was first written; the contract is voided and the injured party has the right to restitution for damages done.

Situations in which the relationship between client and consultant has gone sour can be very troublesome for both parties. Obviously, neither the consultant nor the client 'wins' by demanding the continuation of a consulting assignment in which one or the other is dissatisfied. In such cases it is likely that the consultant will do a less than adequate job and/or the client will provide less than optimal support. Poor quality results can be predicted in either case.

If you are dissatisfied with the performance of your consultant and are considering cancelling the contract, we recommend that, if possible, you call in the consultant for an 'exit interview'. During this interview you should specify how and why you reached the point where you feel that your expectations, needs and preferences have not been met or satisfied. Even though this step may be unpleasant, it is a useful learning opportunity for both you and your consultant.

Modifying a contract due to unexpected and uncontrollable changes in the situation should be readily understood and accepted by both parties, especially if the changed conditions have been identified through the collection and analysis of new data related to the original issues. For instance, one of our recent clients was unable to continue with an assignment because a downturn in the national economy caused a disastrous downturn in the demand for his primary products. It would have been foolish for us to have insisted that the assignment continue, simply because 'we have a contract'. Instead, we helped the client to put the consulting project in mothballs so that it can be reinitiated at an appropriate time in the future.

Because consulting contracts are legal documents, they should always include a statement specifying the circumstances under which they can be altered or cancelled and the agreed process for initiating either action. One element of this statement should specify that 'this contract can be changed only as the result of a face-to-face meeting between the consultant and the client'. In cases where the contract is cancelled, the consultant may have the right to demand fair payment for services already rendered. S/he may also be justified in negotiating payment for income lost due to unanticipated 'down time' created because the contract was cancelled, but it is unethical for the consultant to 'double bill'. That is, s/he should not charge you for lost time that s/he is able to fill by providing billable service to another client organization.

PART III
CHECKLISTS

❖

PREPARATION

Checklist III.1
Preparing for selection interviews

To what degree have the members of your selection committee discussed and arrived at common agreement in response to the following questions? Use the following three-point scale to answer the questions.

3 = We are in **full agreement** as to our requirements in this area.
2 = We are in **considerable agreement** as to our requirements in this area.
1 = We **have significant differences** in how we perceive our requirements in this area.

3 2 1   1. Who needs to be involved in the screening and selection process in order to ensure their support of the selection decision?

3 2 1   2. What, specifically, are our goals for the selection interview in terms of what we will have learned and/or decided about the candidate at the end of the interview?

3 2 1   3. How, specifically, are we going to ensure that we achieve these goals?

3 2 1   4. What specific questions are we going to ask? Who is going to ask them?

3 2 1   5. What might the candidate do or say in response to our questions that would cause us to be concerned about his/her acceptability?

3 2 1   6. Where should the interview be conducted? Why? What are the advantages and disadvantages of alternative interview venues in terms of helping or hindering us in reaching a valid decision?

3 2 1   7. What should we have with us during the interviews to help us to describe our organization and its current situation to the prospective consultants? What is the best way to present this material?

3 2 1   8. What are the worst things that could happen during the selection interview and how can we reduce the risk of their occurrence or most effectively manage them if they do occur?

Checklist III.2
Determining what to tell your consultant

Following is a list of factors that you may choose to reveal to a consultant candidate. Your task is to decide (1) if you should reveal that data to the candidate during the interview and, if so, (2) how it should be presented and (3) by whom. Again, the members of the selection committee should strive to agree on a common answer to each factor. Use the following three-point scale to answer the questions.

3 = We should be **totally open** with our consultant candidates about this factor.

2 = We should provide **only limited information** to our consultant candidates about this factor.

1 = We should provide **no information** to consultant candidates in this area.

3 2 1   1. Information related to the primary problem for which we are considering engaging a consultant.

3 2 1   2. Information related to how this problem is affecting our organization and its intended outputs.

3 2 1   3. Information related to how important this problem is and to whom it is most important.

3 2 1   4. Information related to the most probable consequences of not addressing or dealing with this problem.

3 2 1   5. Information related to the personal stakes key members of our organization may have in our problem, its resolution and/or continuation.

3 2 1   6. Information related to our expectations regarding the consultant and his/her role in dealing with our problem.

3 2 1   7. Information related to what, if anything, we have already done in an effort to deal with the problem and with what results.

3 2 1   8. Information related to our previous experiences with consultants, the types of consultants we have used, what worked well and less well and what, in our perception, contributed to the positive or negative results obtained.

3 2 1   9. Information related to other major events, circumstances or activities currently taking place in our organization and how these might affect the commitment of individuals or groups that might be involved in this consulting effort, the availability of resources for this consulting effort and/or the results of this effort.

3 2 1   10. Information related to the amount of support we, as senior management, are willing to personally commit to the consulting effort, including any limitations or constraints on that support.

3 2 1   11. Information related to the amount of time, energy, resources and budget our organization is willing to invest in order to ensure that this problem situation is dealt with effectively.

3 2 1   12. Information related to our expectations regarding when this consulting effort should begin and expected deadlines for its completion.

3 2 1   13. Information related to our criteria for selecting a consultant for this assignment.

3 2 1   14. Information related to when and how we will make the formal selection of our consultant.

           15. Is there any other information that we should ensure that our consultant candidates are aware of?

           16. Is there any other information that we definitely do not want to reveal to our consultant candidates?

Checklist III.3
Judging the candidate against your selection criteria

The checklists at the conclusion of Part II enabled you to develop your own consultant selection criteria for this assignment. The checklist below is designed to enable you to evaluate each consultant candidate against your selection criteria. You will note that, for simplicity, we have provided only the title of each criterion. We recommend, however, that you ensure that each member of your selection committee have a copy of the detailed selection criteria for ready reference.

We have provided two rating columns for each factor on your selection criteria. The first, in column 2, is to be used for your individual ratings of the degree to which this candidate has demonstrated possession of each selection factor:

4 = This consultant clearly fulfils our needs and requirements in this area.
3 = I have some reservations about this consultant's ability to fulfil our needs and requirements in this area.
2 = I have major reservations about this consultant's ability to fulfil our needs and requirements in this area.
1 = This consultant is clearly not acceptable in this area.

Column 3 is to be used to record the selection committee's final judgement of the degree to which this candidate has demonstrated possession of each selection factor using the following four-point scale:

4 = We agree that this consultant clearly fulfils our needs and requirements in this area.
3 = We have some reservations about this consultant's ability to fulfil our needs and requirements in this area.
2 = We have major reservations about this consultant's ability to fulfil our needs and requirements in this area.
1 = We agree that this consultant is clearly not acceptable in this area.

Factor	Individual rating	Committee rating	Comments

**PROFESSIONAL
CONSULTANT BEHAVIOUR**

1. Treat the organization as the client

2. Focus on the root causes of problems

3. Focus on long-term effects

4. Develop and utilize internal resources

5. Provide help to self-help

6. Focus on practical reality

7. A helicopter perspective

ETHICAL CONSULTANT BEHAVIOUR

1. Maintaining confidentiality

2. Presenting realistic expectations

3. Avoiding conflicting assignments

4. Not recruiting

TECHNICAL COMPETENCE

Our organization is currently
lacking the following knowledge
and specialized skills necessary to
solve/manage this problem
ourselves and, therefore, requires
that they be possessed by the
consultants that we engage (list
specific knowledge and skills below):

Factor	Individual rating	Committee rating	Comments
1.			
2.			
3.			
4.			
5.			
6.			
7.			
8.			

CONSULTING COMPETENCE

1. Analysis and diagnosis

2. Strategic planning

3. Change management

4. Evaluation

INTERPERSONAL COMPETENCE

1. Confrontation skills

2. Risk-taking skills

3. Collaboration

4. Conflict management

5. Relationship building

Factor	Individual rating	Committee rating	Comments

CONSULTING EXPERIENCE

1. The consultant that we engage must have experience dealing effectively with the following types of problem:

2. The consultant that we engage must have experience working at the following organizational levels:

3. The consultant that we engage must have experience working with the following types of organizations and industries:

PERSONAL CHARACTERISTICS

1. Core values

O

O

O

2. Self-confidence

3. Results-oriented

4. Ability to manage personal needs

5. Ability to manage personal style

Checklist III.4
Judging the candidate's responses

Throughout Part III of this book we suggested a number of questions that you could use to help you to bring to the surface essential data about a consultant candidate and his/her probable approach to your problem situation. In the checklist that follows we provide a format for judging each candidate's responses to your questions. We strongly recommend that your selection committee ensure that you are in agreement as to which of the following questions to ask and the answers that you are looking for.

Again, we have included two scales for your use. Use the three-point scale in column 2 to record your individual perceptions of how well the consultant candidate responded to your questions:

3 = I believe that the consultant candidate's responses in this area were **very acceptable**.

2 = I believe that the consultant candidate's responses in this area were **somewhat acceptable**.

1 = I believe that the consultant candidate's responses in this area were **unacceptable**.

Use the three-point scale in column three to record the selection committee's final judgement of how well the consultant candidate responded to your questions:

3 = We agree that this consultant candidate's responses in this area were **very acceptable**.

2 = We agree that the consultant candidate's responses in this area were **somewhat acceptable**.

1 = We agree that the consultant candidate's responses in this area were **unacceptable**.

Factor	Individual rating	Committee rating	Comments
1. How, specifically, did this candidate respond to our request that s/he define his/her goals for the selection interview before we presented our own goals?			

Factor	Individual rating	Committee rating	Comments

2. To what degree did this
    candidate appear to be
    responding openly and
    honestly to our questions as
    opposed to being overly
    guarded and/or holding up a
    façade in order to make a
    good impression?

3. To what degree did this
    candidate appear to be
    'hungry', that is, more interested
    in getting the contract than in
    ensuring that s/he can help us
    to solve our problem situation
    in a cost-beneficial manner.
    (Remember the three warning
    signs of a hungry consultant:
    (1) lots of war stories, (2)
    constantly linking to previous
    clients, and (3) quickly
    prescribing specific solutions
    without probing for problem
    causes.)

4. Did this consultant present a
    diagnostic model that s/he
    would use to analyse our
    problem situation and, if so, is it
    a model that we understand
    and accept?

5. Does this consultant appear to
    have a 'preferred' solution to
    problems, that is, has s/he
    tended to employ the same or
    very similar solutions or measures
    in a majority of his/her
    assignments? Is s/he open to

Factor	Individual rating	Committee rating	Comments
identifying and exploring information that might indicate that other solutions and/or measures may be more appropriate to our specific problem situation?			
6. To what degree does this consultant appear to be selling panaceas and off-the-shelf solutions as opposed to being willing and able to tailor design a solution to our unique situation?			
7. To what degree is this consultant aware of and able to manage the differences between consulting under 'crisis' conditions as opposed to consulting under 'steady state' conditions? Does s/he seem able to shift between the two types of consulting as required by our situation?			
8. To what degree is this consultant willing and able to balance the delivery of task- and process-related interventions, and to shift between the two as required?			
9. To what extent is this consultant likely to solicit and accept input and feedback from key members of our organization?			

Factor	Individual rating	Committee rating	Comments

10. To what degree is this
     consultant willing and able
     to reveal his/her own personal
     confusion and uncertainty and
     to use it to the benefit of the
     consulting assignment?

11. To what degree does this
     consultant have the courage
     to point out and help us to
     deal with unspeakable issues,
     sacred cows, unchallengable
     traditions, and so on?

Checklist III.5
Evaluation of post-interview summaries

Use the three-point scale in column 2 to record your individual perceptions of the consultant candidate's post-interview summary:

3 = I believe that the consultant candidate's summary was **very acceptable** in this area.

2 = I believe that the consultant candidate's summary was **somewhat weak** in this area.

1 = I believe that the consultant candidate's summary was **unacceptably weak** in this area.

Use the three-point scale in column 3 to record your selection committee's final judgement of the consultant candidate's post-interview summary:

3 = We agree that the consultant candidate's summary was **very acceptable** in this area.

2 = We agree that the consultant candidate's summary was **somewhat weak** in this area.

1 = We agree that the consultant candidate's summary was **unacceptably weak** in this area.

Factor	Individual rating	Committee rating	Comments
1. The summary was submitted within the time limit requested.			
2. The summary is written in easy to understand language.			
3. The goals for the consulting assignment presented in the summary clearly reflect our primary concerns and intentions.			
4. The summary clearly demonstrates the consultant candidate's ability to understand the major issues and problems raised during the selection interview.			
5. The summary clearly indicates that the consultant candidate used the selection interview to learn about our organization's strengths and weaknesses relevant to the problem situation.			
6. The summary specifies the additional information that the consultant will need before submitting a formal proposal. It also includes a suggested plan for gathering that information.			
7. The summary contains a list of references which includes the names of organizations in which the consultant candidate has worked with related problems, the nature of the work done, the names of key individuals in those organizations that can be contacted as referees and their telephone numbers.			

EVALUATING PROPOSALS AND CONTRACTS

Checklist III.6
Evaluating the objective contents of proposals

The following checklist can be used to ensure that the consultant's proposal includes the most important elements. We suggest the following rating for each item:

3 = The item is **present** in the proposal and **in good order** (or its absence is acceptable)

2 = The item is **present**, but **needs more work**.

1 = The item is **missing** and should be included

DESCRIPTION OF OUR CURRENT SITUATION

3 2 1   1. The consultant's proposal contains an accurate description of our problem, including a discussion of such key points as why the problem is important, to whom it is important, and so on.

3 2 1   2. The consultant's proposal contains a description of how our problem is impacting on relevant individual, group and/or organizational outputs.

3 2 1   3. The consultant's proposal contains a discussion of what s/he knows about our problem, its causes, impacts, and so on, including a discussion of forces currently acting to support and/or restrain changes in our current situation.

3 2 1   4. The consultant's proposal contains a discussion of measures that we have already taken in an attempt to deal with our problem situation, including the results of those measures and their impact upon the consultant's recommended approach.

3 2 1   5. The consultant's proposal contains a description of any other measures that we have already considered, including a discussion of why these measures have not been implemented.

3 2 1   6. Although the consultant's description of our current situation is clearly based on our own perceptions, it also reflects how the consultant views our situation, including possible incongruencies or discrepancies between the two perceptions.

3 2 1 7. The consultant's proposal makes it clear that the description of the current state presented is 'provisional' and will need to be further investigated, including gathering the perceptions of relevant organizational members and, possibly, of significant stakeholders.

OVERALL PROJECT GOALS

3 2 1 1. The proposal contains a clear description of how we, as the client, want the situation to be at the conclusion of the consulting activity.

3 2 1 2. The proposal states project goals as concise, measurable and achievable targets against which the actual end results of the project can be evaluated.

3 2 1 3. The consultant's proposal presents and discusses the benefits of alternative goals, that is, goals that differ from those that we, as the client, originally presented.

3 2 1 4. The goals presented in the proposal clearly take into consideration any limitations and constraints discussed with the consultant during our pre-proposal meetings.

A PROBLEM ANALYSIS STRATEGY

3 2 1 1. The consultant's proposal includes an assessment strategy designed to ensure that any actions taken are based on a clear, impartial, common view of our problem situation, its impacts and its root causes.

3 2 1 2. The consultant's assessment strategy includes a clarification of the types of data that s/he will require in order to more fully understand our problem situation, specification of what s/he considers to be the best sources of that data, and a clarification of the methods s/he will use to gather information from these sources.

3 2 1 3. The consultant's assessment strategy includes a clarification of how information gathered will be fed back to significant members of our organization.

3 2 1 4. The consultant's proposal clarifies the degree to which s/he will design and facilitate activities intended to help us to use assessment data as the basis for identifying, prioritizing and developing solutions to the causes of our problem situation.

A PROJECT PLAN

3 2 1   1. The consultant's proposal contains a project plan in the form of concise, easily understood steps from problem analysis to submission of his/her final request for payment.

3 2 1   2. Each step in the project plan has its own distinct set of measurable objectives that are clearly linked to the overall goals of the project and to all preceding and following steps.

3 2 1   3. The project plan includes a detailed calendar of events that makes it clear when each step is to begin and when it is expected to be completed.

ROLES AND RESPONSIBILITIES

3 2 1   1. The consultant's proposal clearly defines who is responsible for clerical and administrative tasks and/or costs such as copying and typing.

3 2 1   2. The consultant's proposal clearly defines who is responsible for arranging and paying for venues, meals, lodging, travel, and so on.

3 2 1   3. The consultant's proposal clearly defines which members of the consulting firm are to be involved in this project, in what way, and when.

3 2 1   4. The consultant's proposal clearly defines which individuals or groups from our organization are to be involved in this project, in what way, when, for how long, and so on.

3 2 1   5. The consultant's proposal clearly defines how decisions are to be made relevant to all significant aspects of this project.

3 2 1   6. The consultant's proposal clearly defines the amount and nature of the contact that will be required between the consultant and our organization's senior executives and/or representative – individually or as a group.

3 2 1   7. The consultant's proposal clearly defines who is responsible for evaluating the interim results of this project.

3 2 1   8. The consultant's proposal clearly defines who is responsible for evaluating the final results of this project.

3 2 1   9. The consultant's proposal presents ways to maximize the use of our internal human and physical resources with minimum disruption to prioritized activities and processes.

EVALUATION

3 2 1   1. The consultant's proposal clearly defines specific, measurable mileposts that will be used to ensure that the project is on track.

3 2 1   2. The consultant's proposal clearly defines how achievement of overall project goals will be evaluated to determine the degree to which the end results of the project have met our expectations.

3 2 1   3. The consultant's proposal clearly defines to whom interim and final evaluation results are to be reported.

3 2 1   4. The consultant's proposal clearly defines how decisions will be made regarding an indicated need to alter the original project plan.

FEES AND CHARGES

3 2 1   1. The consultant's proposal includes a specification of his/her fees and charges for each activity described in the project plan.

3 2 1   2. The consultant's proposal clearly defines the terms and conditions relevant to how, when and even if these fees and charges are to be paid.

3 2 1   3. If the consultant is to be paid using a time and expense format, the proposal includes recommendations for a specified discretionary budget that s/he will not exceed without express approval.

3 2 1   4. If the consultant is to be paid using a fixed price format, the proposal includes details which clearly limit the scope of the consultant's activities, the duration of the consulting contract, the costs to our organization and our organization's vulnerability.

Checklist III.7
Evaluating the subjective content of proposals

The following checklist focuses on the approach that the consultant candidate projected in the proposals that s/he submitted. A low rating in any of these items indicates that the candidate may not be appropriate to you and your organization. We suggest the following rating for each item:

3 = The consultant's proposal clearly indicates an **acceptable approach** in this area.

2 = The consultant's approach in this area seems **questionable and should be investigated** further.

1 = The consultant's approach in this area is **unacceptable** and s/he should be rejected.

3 2 1   1. The consultant's proposal indicates that s/he has actively sought ways of reducing project costs by exploring the identification and utilization of our own internal resources.

3 2 1   2. The consultant's proposal indicates that s/he sees his/her job as working in collaboration with the members of our organization in the solution of this and other related problems.

3 2 1   3. The consultant's proposal indicates that s/he is clearly interested in objectively evaluating the ongoing and end results of the consulting project against mutually agreed interim and overall goals and objectives.

3 2 1   4. The consultant's proposal indicates that s/he is able to develop a comprehensive, logically sequenced schedule of events.

3 2 1   5. The consultant's proposal indicates that s/he is willing and able to proactively prepare for problems that might emerge during project implementation.

3 2 1   6. The consultant's proposal indicates that s/he is willing and able to alter his/her action plan in response to unexpected events.

3 2 1   7. The consultant's proposal for evaluation clearly indicates that the intention of his/her proposal is to produce measurable improvements in organizations' results.

3 2 1   8. The consultant's proposal indicates that s/he is skilled at presenting his/her ideas to others.

Checklist III.8
Evaluating consulting contracts

Contracts are a legal confirmation of agreements reached between consultants and their clients through negotiation of the contents of a proposal. Therefore, contracts should, to a large degree, be highly similar to proposals. This checklist focuses primarily on factors where contracts differ from proposals. We suggest the following rating for each item:

3 = The contract is clearly an **acceptable approach** in this area.
2 = The contract is clearly **questionable and should be investigated** further in this area.
1 = The contract is clearly **unacceptable** in this area.

3 2 1   1. The terms and conditions included in the contract are an accurate reflection of the agreements negotiated after reviewing the consultant's proposal.

3 2 1   2. The consulting contract clearly defines conditions and/or situations that may result in a reappraisal and, if necessary, modification of the contract.

3 2 1   3. The consulting contract clearly defines conditions and/or situations that may result in the cancellation of the consulting contract and specifies actions that may be taken should these conditions or situations occur.

3 2 1   4. The consulting contract contains provisions for handling unforeseeable occurrences. That is, both we and our consultant accept the probability that unanticipated difficulties will, inevitably, emerge and that these may deflect attention away from the main issues and delay progress. More importantly, we are both prepared to deal with such difficulties when they occur.

3 2 1   5. The consulting contract is written in a clear, precise and mutually understood language. Although we may have sought legal advice in writing the contract, it can be read, understood and interpreted easily by any relevant non-legal member of our organization.

3 2 1   6. The consulting contract specifies the conditions in which the consultant has the right to demand reimbursement for consulting income lost due to a premature cancellation of the contract or delays in the implementation of components of the action plan.

3 2 1   7. The consulting contract specifies the resources (physical and human) that our organization is expected to commit to this project and we are authorized and willing to commit these resources on behalf of our organization

Checklist III.9
Before you sign the contract

Before agreeing to accept even the best of the proposals that you have received, we recommend that you use the following checklist to ensure that you and key members of your organization are ready and willing to do what is necessary for the change effort to succeed. The rating scale that we recommend for this checklist is as follows:

4 = We are **fully prepared** in this area and should implement the project immediately.

3 = We **need a bit more work** in this area before implementing the project.

2 = We **need much more work** in this area before implementing the project.

1 = We need so much work in this area that we **should consider abandoning the project**.

4 3 2 1   1. **Data collection**: It will be relatively easy for the consultant to gather the data necessary to design, implement and evaluate this project. We are prepared to do what is necessary to enable the consultant to perform this vital function effectively. We are prepared to commit our own and our organization's time, energy and resources to ensure the success of this phase of the consulting project.

4 3 2 1   2. **Acceptability**: We have assessed the acceptability of this project to other stakeholders (for example, unions, potential participants, community residents, and so on). Where project acceptability is low we are prepared to (1) accept the inevitable resistance and/or (2) do what is necessary to reduce or eliminate that resistance, including involving potential resisters in, or informing them of the scope, terms and conditions of this consulting project.

4 3 2 1   3. **Potential for success**: The chances that this consulting project will achieve its stated goals and objectives is reasonably high. Factors essential to the success of the project have been considered and are in place or readily available.

4 3 2 1   4. **Possible risks:** The chances of partial or complete failure of the consulting project have been thoroughly considered, including an identification of factors that are most likely to interfere with, obstruct, or otherwise make it difficult to realize our stated goals and objectives. We have developed contingency plans for eliminating or reducing these factors should they arise.

4 3 2 1   5. **Indirect effects:** We have fully evaluated and are willing to accept possible indirect effects that the full or partial failure of this project may have in such areas as (1) our image with our suppliers, customers, governmental regulators, or owner-financiers; (2) the image of our senior management from the perspective of our middle managers and workers; (3) our ability to design and implement other changes in the future; and (4) our management's credibility in general.

4 3 2 1   6. **Legality:** We are certain that this project does not violate any existing or pending regulations, laws, industry rules or 'guidelines'.

4 3 2 1   7. **Resources:** We have the necessary and sufficient staff, time, facilities, information, knowledge, budget and other resources to maximize the likelihood that this project will be successful.

4 3 2 1   8. **Scheduling:** This project can be scheduled without creating an unduly adverse impact on other scheduled plans or activities within our organization.

4 3 2 1   9. **Short-run costs:** The immediate financial and opportunity costs of this project in terms of material, facilities, staff, and so on, are acceptable.

4 3 2 1   10. **Long-run costs:** The long-run benefits of this project can be objectively projected to exceed the long-term investment in terms of financial and physical resources.

4 3 2 1   11. **Involvement:** Everyone with primary responsibility for implementing any of the various stages of this consulting project has had an opportunity to provide this/her input to the final contract.

IV

MANAGING THE CONSULTANT PROJECT

❖

8

MANAGING AND
EVALUATING CONSULTANTS

❖

This chapter contains concrete suggestions for ensuring that the services provided by your consultant are producing – and continue to produce – the intended results. We begin the chapter with specific suggestions for effectively managing each of the five types of consultants. From there we move on to in-depth techniques for evaluating the ongoing and end results of the consulting project.

MANAGING THE FIVE CONSULTANT TYPES

As discussed in Chapter 2, each of the five types of individuals who call themselves consultants has their own unique approach to the consulting process. As a result, each requires its own form of control and management from you as the client.

MANAGING ACADEMICS

The fact that we do not consider Academics to be consultants does not mean that they do not need to be managed. To the contrary, they may be the most difficult of the so-called consultants to manage for the simple reason that their role is so different. In our experience, most Academics are well aware that the results of their research efforts within your organization can be affected by their perceived relationship with you and other key members of your staff. To ensure the objectivity of their research they will attempt to behave in a manner that ensures that they are perceived as neutral and independent. This may lead to a situation in which they put themselves outside of your control and influence; a condition that is inappropriate under any circumstances.

133

The problem of managing Academics is made more difficult by the simple fact that most managers do not require a contract with Academics doing research in their organizations. If ever there was a situation where a detailed contract should be mandatory, it is with an Academic who calls him/herself a consultant. As with any consulting contract, your contract with an Academic should specify the goals of the project, areas of responsibility, and so on. It should also pay special attention to: (1) the limitations on the Academic's activities, (2) identification of a contact person responsible for actively monitoring the Academic's activities and (3) circumstances in which the Academic must gain approval from his/her contact before acting. The amount of detail that you demand in your contract with an Academic should be inversely proportional to the amount of experience that the Academic has in the 'real world' outside the protective walls of academia. An Academic with little or no experience in the business world should be required to sign a detailed contract and be actively monitored to ensure that they do not 'innocently' meddle in areas that may have serious negative effects on you and your organization.

Case in point

The Managing Director of a highly successful electronics firm saw little danger in allowing a Ph.D. candidate to use his firm's managers and supervisors as a source of data on effective and ineffective leadership behaviours. A month into the research project the MD was confronted by a group who called themselves 'representatives of senior supervisors and middle managers'. This group demanded a meeting with the MD to 'discuss several leadership issues' with which they were dissatisfied. During the meeting the MD discovered that every time the Academic had encountered a condition that didn't meet with his approval he expressed his surprise to the person being observed or interviewed. For example, he had told several supervisors that he was 'very surprised that this organization's senior management has not realized the value of empowering its middle managers and supervisors' and that 'this organization is lagging far behind industry standards in this area'. The more the Academic talked, the more dissatisfied the previously satisfied supervisors and middle managers became.

Because the primary aim of Academics is to achieve insight, understanding or knowledge, they may fail to appreciate that the research they are doing in your organization is interfering with people's ability to perform their assigned task. As a result they may allow their interviews and interactions to be excessively long as they explore topics intended more to satisfy their intellectual curiosity than to contribute to their research goals.

MANAGING HELPING HANDS

Individuals employed as Helping Hands are generally merged with your existing workforce to help you to deal with a short-term overload on existing resources. As a result, managing Helping Hands may require adapting various elements of your normal operating procedures and/or structures. For example, it may be necessary to temporarily expand the physical facilities in which the Helping Hands are to work or redesign existing space to accommodate a temporary expansion in the size of your workforce. The temporary increase of the size and composition of your workforce will also multiply the number and nature of messages that will have to be communicated – up, down and across. This is likely to create a certain amount of confusion and misunderstanding, at least until the permanent and temporary workers become sufficiently familiar with each other to understand the other's language. As a result, it will be necessary to pay special attention to effectively managing information and communications processes.

Increasing the number of people working on the same tasks during any period of raised work volume may also add to the tension level in the workplace, especially if the increase occurs because of or simultaneously with a crisis or emergency situation. Under these conditions, you will need to ensure that affected supervisors are prepared to perform tension-relieving and harmonizing leadership functions. The addition of Helping Hands to an existing workforce often puts a strain on existing supervisory resources. One way of dealing with the temporary demand for extra supervisors is to use it as an opportunity to temporarily assign promising employees to acting supervisor roles. This could become an element of their professional or career development plan. If you adopt this suggestion we further recommend that you place your more experienced supervisors in charge of the Helping Hands.

Because Helping Hands often approach their assignments from a different perspective than do regular, full-time employees they will be less bound by your organization's history and cultural traditions. The negative side of this is that you will have to ensure that conflicts between their perceptions and those of your existing workforce do not reduce current productivity and you will need to guard against the possibility of them creating future problems. The positive side is that the Helping Hands may perceive areas of improvement that you or your internal staff have missed because you are 'too close to the forest'. As a result, it is a good idea to conduct structured exit interviews with Helping Hands to systematically tap into this potentially valuable source of useful information about your organization. In fact, an exit interview is not a bad idea, regardless of the type of consultant you have engaged.

You may experience one additional problem when engaging Helping Hands. Because they are usually 'rented' through firms specializing in temporary office and/or managerial staff, their fees are typically anywhere from two to five times as much as regular employees performing the same tasks. This may cause understandable resentment from your regular employees.

MANAGING TRAINING CONSULTANTS

Most competent Training Consultants are prepared to design, create and deliver a wide range of lectures, seminars, courses or workshops. However, it would be naïve and irresponsible to assume that you can delegate training activities to Training Consultants and then forget them; which is what happens all too often! If you engage a Training Consultant you must be prepared to invest considerable time, attention and energy before, during and after the training events to ensure that the desired outcomes of the training programme are realized.

One of your earliest challenges is balancing your perceptions of the training needs of your organization's members against the amount and value of resources that you are willing and able to commit to meeting those needs. Most individuals who call themselves competent, qualified Training Consultants will suggest that you begin with a 'training needs assessment'. That advice is usually excellent, unless you are absolutely positive that you have already identified a high priority training need. For example, if your vehicle accident rate is 30 per cent higher than the industry average despite the fact that your vehicles are new and well maintained, it is reasonable to assume that driver training is in order.

If you agree with your consultant's recommendation to conduct a training needs assessment, make sure that what you get is really a training *needs* assessment as opposed to a training *wants* assessment. The difference is more than merely semantic. Far too many so-called consultants conduct training needs assessments by gathering data about the training that people in various positions believe they need. The data gained often shows some interesting trends, most of which are meaningless. For example, a needs assessment conducted for a large manufacturing company in a third world country indicated that 65 per cent of all clerical and administrative employees 'needed' more training in 'computer utilization'. That was a bit surprising in light of the fact that the company had few computers and no plans for expanding its IT capacity. Why did so many employees want the training? So that they would be more attractive when they applied for positions in more advanced organizations.

A proper training needs analysis will begin by examining the jobs that people do. The competent Training Consultant will ask, 'To what degree are incumbents in these jobs currently producing the outputs expected of them?' If the answer indicates that outputs are currently falling below expectations, or are likely to do so at some time in the future, the Training Consultant will ask a second question: 'To what degree is the gap between actual and intended outputs a direct result of a lack of skills, as opposed to being caused by other factors (such as old equipment, poor structures, low motivation)?' If the answer to this question indicates that the cause of the problem is a lack of skills, the consultant will then ask, 'Can we improve incumbent skills at a cost that is less than the cost of the gap between actual and intended outputs?' Only if the answer to the last question is 'Yes' should the consultant be authorized to design and implement a training effort. If the answer is 'No' then you may want to consider such options as living with the gap, bringing in Helping Hands to show your incumbents how to perform more effectively, or outsourcing the tasks.

Once the training programme has been designed and is being implemented, you will need to monitor its progress to determine whether it is likely to close, or at least reduce, the identified skills gap. No matter how effective the training programme, you cannot expect participants to perform in a flawless manner immediately following their training. The development of proficiency requires practice, willingness to take risks and an ability to learn from experience. Even useful competencies are vulnerable to being discarded if you and your managers do not ensure that recently trained individuals are actively supported upon returning to their workplace. This will include ensuring that newly acquired competencies are at least tolerable if not fully acceptable to the participants' co-workers.

Case in point

Many years ago one of our academic colleagues conducted a research project for a large department store chain to find out why newly employed clerks were not using the sales and customer service skills that they had been taught as part of their induction training programme. A profile of trainees revealed that most were single females aged 18 to 21. A profile of the department store's 'typical' clerk indicated that most were divorced or widowed females between the ages of 50 and 60. Our colleague went so far as to say that most existing clerks were very 'grandmotherly' in appearance.

Imagine his shock when he discovered that newly assigned trainees were being coached by their more matronly colleagues to 'slow down so that our bosses won't expect too much of us'. Those trainees who continued to react promptly to customers entering the store or to do 'unnecessary' tasks such as putting stock in order were severely cautioned by the older women to 'be careful not to upset the apple cart'. If the trainee continued to be motivated despite the clear warnings, they became the victims of mysterious 'accidents'. For example, a drawer at the bottom of a display counter would open or a heavy rack of clothing would tip just as an eager young clerk was 'racing' by to greet a customer. In more than one case the young girls experienced painful injuries. And guess who was responsible for setting these dangerous traps. That's right – granny!

It is not unusual for co-workers to apply various forms of coercive pressure to convince the training participants to revert to their old, familiar, comfortable work patterns and practices after returning to the workplace. Under such conditions, you must be prepared to provide clear, non-ambiguous and persistent encouragement and support to training participants. In the worst case, you may have to clearly insist that all supervisors and co-workers actively support training participants' efforts to apply their newly acquired competencies to the ongoing, real-life operations of their work situation. It may even be necessary to extend the scope of the Training Consultant's assignment to allow him/her to follow their former training course participants back to the workplace where they can provide follow-up assistance with application problems.

MANAGING EXPERT CONSULTANTS

Expert Consultants are typically tasked to work with relative autonomy, managing their own activities from the initial situational diagnosis through to the submission of their final report and recommendations. Many Expert Consultants are unwilling or unable to take a broad, system-wide perspective to the work that they do in organizations. Often, they don't recognize that their work, no matter how narrow, is likely to cause reverberations within and/or between other significant organizational functions. To maintain control in such situations, it is wise to place the consultant under the supervision of a respected line manager who is reasonably knowledgeable in the consultant's area of specialization. The supervising manager should actively monitor the interface between the consultant and other key systems and functions within the organization. In addition, s/he should ensure that all work performed by the consultant is in full agreement with the goals, terms, conditions and expectations detailed in the consulting contract.

It is not unusual for Expert Consultants to submit excellent recommendations that are resisted or rejected by the members of the client organization responsible for their implementation. The most common cause of this problem is that organization members feel that they have had insufficient opportunity to be involved in or to influence the consultant's recommendations. To avoid this, the Expert Consultant's supervising manager should ensure that key members of the organization are provided with sufficient opportunity to interact with, provide input to and influence the Expert Consultant while his/her recommendations are being developed. S/he should also ensure that the consultant listens to and gives fair consideration to the input received.

MANAGING PROCESS CONSULTANTS

Although the role, functions and potential contributions of Process Consultants seem to be increasingly understood and accepted, many organization leaders still know too little about what they do and how they do it. In the absence of information or experience with Process Consultants, it is natural to expect them to behave similarly to Expert Consultants. As a result you may be surprised by several aspects of Process Consultants' behaviour that differ significantly from any other type of consultant. For example:

1. A Process Consultant is likely to require that you and your senior managers become active 'partners' in the consulting effort. In fact, s/he is likely to propose strategies and tactics that will put you, your managers and other members of your organization in the forefront throughout the consulting process. Although this is usually necessary if the Process Consultant is to be of maximum benefit, your executives may resent being drawn away from operative duties. This is very likely if these executives consider their tasks to be of higher priority than the change effort or perceive their involvement as unnecessary, time-consuming steps in the process.

2. Rather than allowing themselves to be treated as subordinates, Process Consultants are likely to behave as peers to your organization's most senior executives and, as a result, are likely to stongly resist being 'delegated to'.

3. Throughout the assignment a Process Consultant is likely to continually confront you and your organization's management with requests for decisions related to specific aspects of the consulting assignment. These could include requests to modify or expand the scope and/or alter the methodology of the consulting assignment resulting from the new data gained during the consultant's ongoing work with the organization.

4. Process Consultants' tendency to directly confront executives with unpleasant 'truths' often results in them being seen as insubordinate and undisciplined by many executives, especially those used to very formal hierarchical structures.

It is important that you and the members of your organization understand that all of the preceding behaviours by a Process Consultant result from their underlying belief that successful change efforts require the following four basic, essential factors:

1. They are built on a collaborative consulting relationship in which the consultant and the senior managers of the client organization *share* responsibility for the success of the change effort.

2. They require a flexible consulting focus that is proactively responsive to emerging conditions and newly discovered information.

3. They require significant involvement in, understanding of and commitment to the consulting effort on behalf of those organizational members responsible for implementing or impacted by that effort.

4. They have an overall goal of increasing the organization's capacity to deal effectively with similar or related issues in the future by ensuring that organization managers and members learn from the problem-solving processes implemented today.

Process Consultants are well aware that being surrounded by crocodiles is far less dangerous than the long-term costs of failing to drain the swamp. More importantly, they are aware that many of the managers with whom they work may understand that perception intellectually, but will still reach for a club at the first sighting of a crocodile. As a result, truly competent Process Consultants have learned to be 'appropriately manipulative'. For example, they may hide your clubs so that you are forced to focus on draining the swamp.

The basic beliefs of Process Consultants often result in them being seen as a 'thorn under the saddle' of busy executives who expect their consultants to give them the answers as opposed to asking them questions. However, when used in the right situation, it is the questions that will lead to long-term organizational improvement – not the answers.

Our advice for avoiding misunderstandings about the way a Process Consultant goes about his/her job is to provide the consultant with an opportunity to facilitate an information meeting for the members of your organization with whom s/he will be working. During this meeting the consultant can clarify issues such as working methods, underlying beliefs and assumptions, expectations, and so on.

CONSULTANT EVALUATION

The topic of evaluation is not separate from the preceding suggestions for how to effectively manage consultants. On the contrary; evaluation is, or at least should be, an integral part of your overall consultant management strategy. You and your organization engage consultants on the assumption that they will directly or indirectly increase the ability of your organization to attain some predefined goals or objectives. The specific goals and objectives that you expect to reach as a direct result of the efforts of your consultant should be specified, negotiated, understood and accepted by all involved parties *before* the consultation process is actually begun. Because they are part of a contractual agreement, you are entitled and, in fact, obligated to develop and maintain documented verification of the degree to which the goals defined in the consulting contact are being met at any point during or after the consulting effort.

The importance of evaluation as an integral step in any consulting effort cannot be overemphasized. Regardless of the size of your organization, there are likely to be a number of parties who will expect you and your consultant to be able to justify the 'value' of the consulting effort. These parties may include unions, supervisors, managers, staff personnel, your board of directors, suppliers, shareholders, customers, regulating agencies, and so on.

WHAT IS 'OF VALUE'?

The meaning of the word 'value' is highly subjective. However, most people intuitively evaluate the 'value' of consulting services in terms of the degree to which these services satisfy their own vested individual interests. As a result, different people will take different positions regarding the 'value' of any given service.

Case in point

One of the authors was Coordinator for a team of eight consultants working for the Executive Director of Nuclear Power Operations and his Project Director in the construction of a nuclear power plant. The costs for this consulting team were considerable: $9,375 per day or $2.25 million per year, plus annual expenses of about 15 per cent of fees. During a preliminary on-site inquiry, the Public Service Commissioners responsible for monitoring the cost-benefit of the project questioned the legitimacy of spending over $2.5 million a year for a team of consultants. They asked, 'What value do these people add to the project?' The Project and Executive Directors responded with a long list of the contributions they believed that the team was generating, including: (1) improved communication of more timely, accurate and comprehensive information; (2) an improved ability to recognize and deal with the inevitable misunderstandings and conflicts; (3) an improved quality of the decisions which are then implemented with greater acceptance and commitment; and (4) better coordination and integration of the work activities performed by each of the different departments, functions and companies working on the project.

The commissioners replied: 'That's all soft stuff. We still don't understand: What *real value* do the consultants add to the project?' The Executive Director tried again: 'Our consultants help all contributors to the project to work together more productively, more safely, and with greater trust in each other.' 'Well, that sounds good.' replied the commissioners, 'but, bottom line, can you tell us how all this fluff translates into the *value* which the consultants are adding to this project?'

The Project Director finally realized what the Commission was looking for. That is, he finally understood what would have *value* for them and said, 'As you know, this project costs about $1.75 million per day. The consulting team helped us to save about 24 days during the first nine months of this year. That's about $42 million in savings that we can attribute directly to their efforts so far. The consulting team will cost us no more than $2.6 million for the entire year. As a result, we have a bottom line saving of at least $39.4 million thanks to their efforts.'

It is in your self-interest to be quite clear about the intended 'value' of the results of any type of consultation that you authorize or initiate. In the preceding case, the 'value' which the Public Service Commissioners ultimately accepted was the *dollar value* of time saved. An explanation of the 'value' of the consulting team to different interest groups with different sets of 'valued results' might require the Project Director to stress the consulting team's contribution in different terms, that is, he will have to speak their 'language'.

WHAT TO EVALUATE

There are five possible levels at which you might evaluate the contributions of a consultant. These are:

O   **Level 1:** Did participants *enjoy* the activity?
O   **Level 2:** Did participants *learn* the skills and/or concepts intended by the activity?
O   **Level 3:** Were participants *able to apply* their newly learned skills and/or concepts in the performance of their jobs?
O   **Level 4:** Were participants *allowed to apply* their newly learned skills and/or concepts in the performance of their jobs?
O   **Level 5:** Did the training or consulting effort make *any real difference* in the effectiveness of the organization?

We devote the remainder of this chapter to a discussion of each of these five levels of evaluation and the goals that they infer for consulting and training activities.*

Level 1: *To what extent did participants enjoy the training and/or the consultation activity?* Far too often, consultants focus their evaluation efforts on organizational members' level of *satisfaction* with an activity and little more. We refer to this type of evaluation as 'happy-face' evaluations; a reference to (1) the evaluation criteria which often consist of counting the number (and size) of the smiles on participants' faces after the activity as well as to (2) the method frequently used to collect and report participant ratings, namely, a graduated series of cartoons ranging from a big, bright 'happy face' to a dark, gloomy 'frowny face'.

Happy-face evaluations usually consist of short questionnaires to be completed by participants at the conclusion of a course, programme or consultation. These questionnaires typically ask such summary questions as: What did you like most? What did you like least? Was the consultant or trainer interesting? Did s/he speak clearly and use language that you understood? If we were to do this again, what would you like the consultant or trainer to do differently? Would you recommend this course, programme or process to others? Questionnaires may also ask participants to assess the training or consultation venue, the quality of meals and

---

* Our presentation of the five levels of evaluation is a modified form of the work of Donald L. Kirkpatrick (1994), *Evaluating Training Programs: The Four Levels*. San Francisco: Berret-Koehler Publishers.

refreshments, the ease of commuting and parking, the relevance of materials presented, the effectiveness of the methods used, and so on. Participants may even be asked to compare this experience with others in which they have participated.

If the only purpose of an evaluation exercise is to provide consultants or trainers with immediate feedback on their personal contributions to the consulting activity or course, we might conclude that a happy-face approach to evaluation is, in a limited (and limiting) way, more or less adequate. Unfortunately, the desire for good ratings may cause consultants and trainers to avoid topics during the activity that could evoke negative reactions from influential participants. They may also avoid dealing with significant content that could be difficult for participants to understand or master. Similarly, consultants and trainers may be overly cautious in confronting organizational members, even when such confrontation might be exactly what is needed to increase the long-term effectiveness of the effort. While we understand the temptation to design and implement activities with the goal of eliciting positive ('happy face') results, we firmly believe that consultants and trainers are obliged to risk their own popularity in the service of meeting the agreed goals and objectives of the activity. We strongly believe that consultants are not hired to be liked; they are hired to make a positive difference in your organization's output

Level 2: *To what extent have participants reached or exceeded the intended learning objectives established for the training or consulting activity?* There are numerous methods for testing whether or not participants have learned the information, knowledge or conceptual theories presented to them. The most familiar method is the paper-and-pencil examination format we all experienced daily while attending school. Although such tests may be expedient means by which to evaluate a student's acquisition of knowledge, they do little to evaluate a participant's ability to apply this knowledge in real-life work situations. For example, an individual's ability to list the six most essential characteristics of an effective corporate strategy (as taught in an MBA programme) may have little relationship to that individual's ability to mobilize an organization's key executives and facilitate a process through which an effective corporate strategy can be formulated and agreed upon.

If the purpose of evaluation activities is to 'test' which employees derive the most versus least from exposure to the same learning opportunities, then Level 2 evaluations are, perhaps, the most appropriate. However, if the intent of the consultation or course is to increase participants' applicable proficiency, then other evaluation methods must be utilized.

Level 3: *To what extent are participants able to actually apply their learning to improve their performance of the tasks that are inherent in their jobs?* We consider this to be the minimum acceptable level for evaluating most consulting or training efforts. If a consultant is truly competent, s/he will usually suggest some form of

Level 3 evaluation even before the question of evaluation is raised. If s/he doesn't, it is time to start wondering about his/her competence, experience, or motives. An appropriate way of conducting Level 3 evaluations is to provide participants with an opportunity to demonstrate the application of their knowledge in a 'real-world' environment. For example, in courses in automechanics, students are required to demonstrate their ability to dismantle and rebuild a motor.

Real-world evaluations are often relatively easy to construct for tangible subjects such as automechanics, but can be difficult for more abstract subjects such as strategic planning. However, they are not impossible to develop and, in fact, are far easier to develop today than ever before. For example, the use of modern computer simulations offers a world of opportunity for testing the application of abstract concepts in situations that are often (frighteningly) close to the real world. Another alternative is the creation of classroom environments that model the 'real world'. For example, many hotel and restaurant training programmes maintain fully functional kitchens and restaurants which prepare food for and serve real customers in an environment that is as close to reality as one can get.

Level 4: *To what extent are participants allowed to apply their learning once they return to their jobs?* There is nothing more frustrating for a truly professional consultant than seeing highly motivated, skilled individuals returning to their workplaces intending to do things differently, only to find that they are subjected to extreme pressures to do things as they did before attending their training. In some cases these pressures come from co-workers who have not had the opportunity to gain the insights provided by the training programme. In other cases, it comes from supervisors who feel threatened by their subordinates' new skills or knowledge. Whatever the reason, the result is the same; within weeks participants return to their old, habitual ways of doing things.

If you want to achieve Level 4 results, your best action is to ensure that the programme design includes the ongoing follow-up support necessary to maximize the application of learning after the training. Such support includes:

O   The application of learning should be written into participants' job descriptions, performance goals and performance evaluations.

O   Managers and supervisors should be required and enabled to consistently and persistently serve as models for using the new concepts and skills. Of course, this means that the organization's executives, managers and supervisors will have to acquire sufficient proficiency in these competencies to enable them to function as *credible* models.

O   Mentoring and on-site consultations should be established to coach, encourage, prompt and provide feedback.

O   Obstacles to the application of new learning should be identified in advance and every effort made to remove or manage them.

O   Formal and informal incentives should be established to encourage and
        acknowledge members who have applied their newly learned skills and
        techniques.

Level 5: *Did the training or consulting activity make any real, positive difference
in the effectiveness of your organization?* This is what we call the 'so what' level of
evaluation. Let's face it. You don't sponsor consulting or training activities to make
people feel good, to teach them skills, or to improve their individual performance.
You sponsor them in order to improve the effectiveness or productivity of your
organization or one or more of its functions/units. As a result, any consulting or
training activity funded by your organization should have this level as its ultimate
goal.

It is possible for a training or consulting activity to receive excellent Level 1 to 4
evaluations without making any positive difference whatsoever to your organization's performance! For example, we know of an organization that spent several
hundred thousand pounds on a comprehensive 'Customer Focus Programme'.
Management was pleased with post-course evaluations which indicated that participants (1) thoroughly enjoyed the course, (2) were able to demonstrate that
they had learned the skills required of them, (3) were applying these skills in their
daily work and (4) were fully supported in their efforts to apply those skills. When
we convinced the organization to examine Level 5 results they were shocked to
discover that the programme had resulted in few measurable increases in either
sales, revenues or profits. In fact, when the firm's customers were asked about the
benefits of the programme, their first reaction was to comment on the disruption
to service that they had experienced while the programme was being conducted.
More importantly, it was clear that the costs of the programme had far exceeded
the value of any possible tangible or intangible benefits.

There are a number of approaches to conducting Level 5 evaluations. The most
obvious of these is to assess the impacts which the consulting or training effort
has had upon your organization's current critical performance indicators, which
might include positive changes in such factors as:

O   costs (labour, materials, financing, etc.);
O   grievances (customer, union, supplier, regulatory agencies, etc.);
O   quality (returns, rejects, credits, etc.);
O   productivity (time, quantities, in-process delays, etc.);
O   personnel (absenteeism, turnover, competency levels, etc.);
O   economic ratios;
O   safety;
O   maintenance;
O   and so on.

In addition, the results of employee or customer opinion surveys before and after
the intervention can be compared to identify changes resulting from a consulting

effort. In our experience a comparison of pre- and post-activity assessments can provide excellent data when used judiciously. Be careful, however, because they can also provide grossly misleading results when interpreted by naïve, inexperienced evaluators.

Case in point

A group of consultants began their assignment with a large client organization by distributing a comprehensive survey to be completed by all of the organization's employees. The results of this survey were analysed by the consultants and the senior managers of the client organization and a number of specific problem areas were identified and prioritized. One problem area identified was that there appeared to be poor cooperation between the organization's interdependent functions. This item was rated at 3.8 on a 6-point scale, where 6 would indicate an exceptionally high degree of satisfaction.

Based on survey results, the consulting team designed and facilitated a number of interventions, one of which was specifically focused on increasing the cooperation between interdependent functions. The consulting team was pleased to note that their two-day 'Interfunctional Cooperation Workshop' was one of the most popular and appreciated of the interventions that they implemented (that is, it received excellent Level 1 evaluations). After six months, the initial survey was readministered to evaluate the effects that the consulting effort had had upon the prioritized problem areas that the initial survey had indicated. Both the client and the consulting team were shocked and distressed when one of the lowest ratings on the second survey was given to cooperation between interdependent functions. It had gone from a 3.8 on the first survey to a 3.1 on the second survey. As the client expressed it, 'Jeez, it looks like you guys made things worse instead of better!'

The consultants in the above case made the critical mistake of assuming that the two surveys were identical. That is not so surprising in light of the fact that they used an identical survey form which contained identical instructions and was administered to exactly the same people. However, they missed the simple fact that the questions were not identical in the eyes and minds of their respondents. The first time the respondents filled in the survey form, their answers to the questions related to interfunctional cooperation were based on a relatively limited, naïve view of the topic. Thanks to the workshop, respondents' insight into the nature and value of interfunctional cooperation was drastically increased. In addition, they were provided with concrete evidence of their own inability to effectively cooperate over functional boundaries. As a result, when presented with the second survey, they were much more critical and demanding.

ONGOING EVALUATION OF THE CONSULTING EFFORT

Many clients, and their consultants, make the critical mistake of waiting until the conclusion of a consulting effort before formally evaluating its results. We prefer a continuous evaluation process that is initiated at the start and carries through to the conclusion of the consulting effort. Such evaluations enable you and your consultants to identify opportunities to expedite the process or to discover new, more productive or profitable alternative tactics for reaching your strategic change objectives.

Continuous evaluation means that every major step in the consultant's action plan should include a milepost against which you and your consultant can compare the progress of the effort in terms of such factors as:

O   Is your initial plan unfolding as originally intended?

O   Is the effort producing the expected results?

O   Is the effort on schedule?

O   Have any unexpected events occurred or conditions arisen that may have impacted on project results?

O   Do the unexpected events or conditions make it necessary for you to revise or adjust your initial plan, strategy or tactics?

O   Do the unexpected events or conditions reveal previously hidden problems or create new problems that require you to divert resources from the original consulting effort?

O   What unintended side-effects, if any, has the change effort created and what, if anything, should you do about them?

O   Are you getting what you expected from your consultant? If not, what do you want to do about it?

You, as the client, may believe that positive answers to the above questions are enough to warrant patting the consultant on the back and letting him/her continue. However, attainment of positive short-term results is not the only criterion against which you should judge your consultant's performance. Following is a list of questions that are more 'process-oriented'. That is, they look more specifically at the behaviour and methods your consultant is using as s/he works with you and other members of your organization:

1.   What new knowledge, skills, insights have you, your managers and/or other members of your organization gained as the result of the consultant's contributions?

2.   In what ways are you, your managers and other members of your organization behaving differently as the result of your consultant's contributions?

3. How are you, your managers and/or other members of your organization responding to your consultant and his/her contributions?

4. How would you describe the client–consultant relationship? In what ways is it satisfactory? How can it be improved?

5. How much influence does your consultant have over you, your managers and other members of your organization? How is that influence being exerted? To what effect?

6. What methods, techniques and activities is the consultant utilizing in his/her interventions?

7. To what degree do you, your managers and/or others in your organization understand and feel comfortable with your consultant's methods, techniques, and activities?

8. To what degree does your consultant appear to understand and respect the culture of your organization, including its norms and taboos? To what extent does s/he conform to your organizational culture as opposed to appropriately challenging traditional norms and taboos?

9. To what degree does your consultant stay focused on the specific task, problem and/or issues for which s/he was engaged as opposed to engaging (or inviting organization members to engage in) trivial or irrelevant side issues?

10. To what degree is your consultant actively seeking and receptive to relevant but previously hidden issues that might enable you and your managers to modify the focus of the project in an appropriate and useful manner?

11. How would you describe your management's role in the consulting project? As partners? Junior partners? Evaluators? Supervisors? Critics? Uninvolved? To what degree is that role appropriate?

12. How would you describe the roles of other key members of your organization with regard to the project? How appropriate are those roles?

13. To what degree has your consultant initiated efforts to engage the members of your organization to actively participate in the consulting project?

14. To what degree does your consultant maintain a 'helicopter' perspective? Equally important, does s/he know when and how to come down to earth?

15. Are the results identified in questions 1–14 acceptable to the management and other members of the organization?

16. Who or what is influencing any negative responses to questions 1–15?

17. What, specifically, should be changed in the way your consultant has been working with you and your organization?

18. What, specifically, should be changed in the way you, your executives or any other members of your organization have been working on this change effort?

19. What, specifically, should be changed in the basic consulting agreement?

EVALUATION OF THE END RESULTS OF A CONSULTING EFFORT

To paraphrase a story told by Robert Mager,* a client asked a prospective consultant, 'How can I evaluate the value of your contributions to my organization?' The consultant replied, 'The most valuable effects of my work are intangible and are therefore impossible to measure.' The client responded by suggesting that the consultant's fees be paid in the same currency – intangibly! We would be the first to admit that it can be extremely difficult to objectively evaluate the end results achieved as a direct result of a consultant's efforts, but it is seldom *impossible*.

Case in point

One of the authors was called upon to help resolve a conflict between the police chief and fire chief in a small city. The mayor, who had called in the consultant, gave the following explanation for how the conflict had begun. One day last year there was a motor accident in town. The collision was so violent that both vehicles caught fire. The fire chief and police chief arrived at the same time and immediately began to argue over who was in charge. The argument became extremely heated, with each chief publicly expressing uncensored evaluations of the other personality and performance. Since this less than auspicious beginning, the conflict had steadily worsened. At the time the consultant was called in, the two chiefs were refusing to speak to each other, refusing to attend meetings together, and engaging in mudslinging both within their organizations and in the public media.

The mayor in the above case asked the consultant, 'How will I know if you have been successful in resolving the conflict between my police and fire chiefs?' Mager's consultant might have answered, 'The results of my efforts in this assignment can't be measured objectively. You'll "know in your gut" if I have succeeded!' Using our technical language, we conclude that this is a 'bullshit answer from a lazy consultant'! Our answer to the mayor began with a question: 'What are the primary problems being caused by the conflict between the two chiefs?' Her answer included such factors as having to make the same presentation twice because they would not attend meetings together; increased complaints from the members of each chief's department; non-productive meetings; and negative reactions from taxpayers.

Based on the mayor's answers we formulated several provisional goals for the consulting intervention. These were presented first to the mayor and, then,

* Robert F. Mager and Peter Pipe (1970), *Analyzing Performance Problems*, or 'You really Oughta Wanna'. Belmont, CA: Fearon Publishers.

privately to each of the two chiefs. With some modification, all parties agreed to commit ourselves to the following criteria against which the success of the change effort would be evaluated:

As the result of this consulting effort:
○   the two chiefs will jointly identify areas of overlapping or unclear responsibility and, together with the mayor, will agree on how these areas are to be managed in the future.
○   the number of complaints from members of the chiefs' respective departments related to the conflict will be reduced by 50 per cent within two months and by 90 per cent within six months.
○   each chief will demonstrate, to the mayor's satisfaction, that he respects and actively attempts to understand the other's views during meetings with the mayor.
○   neither chief will make derogatory remarks about the other in public settings.

The preceding specific goals for the consulting effort served two major purposes. First, and most obviously, they provided a basis upon which the results of the consulting effort could be evaluated. Second, and less obviously, the process of engaging all involved parties to establish mutually beneficial and acceptable goals made it clear that the good faith and active commitment of all parties was a prerequisite to reaching the desired results. Without the active commitment of the two chiefs, there was little chance of conducting a successful change effort.

9

CHANGE MANAGEMENT

❖

We can't run or hide from the need for change. Changing social, economic, political and technical developments on a global scale assure us that change in all aspects of our lives will persist in increasing volume and intensity. The reverberations that these changes will continue to create in our work and personal lives are unavoidable. As a result, one of the most important characteristics of healthy, high performing organizations today is that they are doing what is necessary to ensure that they are healthy and high performing tomorrow. To do this, they are permeated by a culture of effective change management from top to bottom. The senior managers of such organizations are well aware that change management is an integral part of their jobs and are both willing and able to proactively consider changing not only the products and services that their organization creates and delivers but also the way people work, the way machines are operated, the way systems and procedures are designed, installed and managed, and so on.

Many of the changes that people in organizations are being forced to deal with produce powerful emotional reactions. Many of them feel alone and possibly isolated. Others feel that they have been betrayed by those whom they trusted to protect them and provide security. Senior executives and managers have a responsibility to anticipate the emotional turbulence created by change and the processes through which organizational members are likely to respond. In short, they must have the skills necessary to effectively manage the people-side of complex organizational change. That means, first and foremost, that they must rid their organizations of such simplistic and false beliefs about change as, *'you can't teach an old dog new tricks'*.

The simple fact is that people, regardless of their ages, are constantly changing. There are, however, great differences in how they respond to the demand for a specific change:

○   Sometimes they choose to accept and support change and sometimes they choose to reject and resist it.

○   Sometimes the process of change is so slow that neither those changing nor close observers such as their bosses, peers, subordinates, friends, or family members are consciously aware of the changes that are taking place. Sometimes change is so rapid and dramatic that it is clearly evident to those who change *and* to those who are affected by or observe the changes.

○   Sometimes people think they are changing, but the change occurs more in their self-perceptions than in their actual thinking, feelings or behaviours. Sometimes they do not want to change, but want others to think they are changing. Therefore, what they change is their façade – for example, how they appear or sound – with no corresponding internal changes in their personal beliefs, values, attitudes or priorities.

Because organizations are composed of, operated, maintained and led by people, virtually anything that might be said about individuals applies equally well to organizational change:

○   Organizations can change (or simply appear to change) their public images (appearance); visions, missions, strategies of systems (thinking); philosophies, attitudes or values (feelings); supervisory practices, technologies, work methods, leadership styles, or patterns and styles of communicating (behaviours).

○   Such changes may be made on the basis of either explicit, conscious informed choice, or implicit, non-conscious, unrecognized choice

○   Such changes may be slow and steady or rapid and chaotic. Slow change is often experienced as 'evolutionary' and is usually accepted or tolerated by those who prefer the current state and experienced as too slow by those who believe that they are undeservedly suffering under present conditions. Rapid change is often experienced as 'revolutionary' and is usually welcomed by persons who feel disadvantaged by current conditions but it is typically resisted by those whose positions of power and influence may be threatened by changes in those conditions.

○   And any specific change may be met with ready acceptance and support and/or frustration and active resistance.

DEALING POSITIVELY WITH RESISTANCE TO CHANGE

Many consultants and managers hold the *optimistic view* that people, by nature, welcome change and will typically change themselves whenever they perceive an opportunity to improve their current condition. Others hold the *pessimistic view* that people are, by nature, conservative and reluctant to change and do so only when they can no longer resist. Which view is true? *Both!* Many people, and many organizations, seem to thrive on change. They constantly seek new opportunities, new methods, new behaviours, new products, and so on. While other people, and organizations, seem to invest most of their energy trying to ignore or avoid the demands and opportunities for change. In so doing they employ a variety of tactics to preserve and maintain the conditions with which they are most familiar and comfortable.

Within organizations, change-seekers and change-resisters often hold polarized views of one another. Change-seekers often describe change-resisters as 'fossils' who are likely to drive the organization into bankruptcy by not responding promptly and proactively to changing conditions in the marketplace. Change-resisters often describe change-seekers as 'loose cannons' who are out to destroy the organization's stability and traditions. When change-seekers and change-resisters join forces, each can benefit from the other's strengths which compensate for their own 'blind spots'. For example, change-resisters may act to slow down the change process and prevent change-seekers from taking impulsive actions. Change-seekers may prompt change-resisters to respond more rapidly in times of uncertainty. Cooperation between change-seekers and change-resisters can also reduce the possibility that either will overuse their weaknesses, and cause the change process to occur too rapidly or too slowly.

In an excellent article on managing resistance to change, Karp* points out that managers and consultants often respond inappropriately to those who they perceive as resisting change, especially if it is a change that they are personally promoting. When faced with resistance, they typically use one or more of the following oppositional strategies to deal with it:

1. *Breaking down the resistance* by threatening, coercing, selling, or aggressive reasoning.
2. *Avoiding resistance* through deflection, 'not hearing' it or attempting to induce guilt.
3. *Discounting resistance* by labelling it as unimportant, devaluing the level of awareness of the resister, or appealing to the resister's need to conform.

Although these strategies may work to some degree in the short term, they rarely provide lasting positive support for the change effort and are often quite costly in the long term. For example, the use of threats and attempts to induce guilt may produce even more intense resistance at a later time, to a completely different change activity. Karp suggests a more positive approach to resistance that is based on two basic assumptions:

* H.B. Karp (1988). 'A Positive Approach to Resistance', in *The 1988 Annual: Developing Human Resources.* La Jolle, CA: University Associates. pp. 143–6.

1. *Resistance 'is'*. People will always resist, knowingly or not, those things that they do not perceive as in their best self-interest.
2. *Resistance should be honoured.* Because resistance is a normal human reaction, people who resist should be dealt with in a respectful manner.

The first step in Karp's approach is to *bring to surface the resistance* that exists within your organization to a proposed change effort. This involves first making the expression of resistance as 'safe' as possible. Once resisters are aware that they are not going to be attacked or punished for their views, it is far easier to surface the real reasons for their resistance. One of the best methods for surfacing resistance is to simply ask for it.

Once resistance has been surfaced, it must be *honoured*. This involves honestly communicating an attitude that resistance is a vital source of information which can reveal potential problems in the change process. Honouring resistance also means respecting the individual's right to feel as they do and actively listening to their opinions and feelings. It may even mean rewarding resisters for daring to make their views public.

The next step in Karp's approach is to actively *explore the resistance*, which involves probing to identify what, exactly, is causing it. This step recognizes the simple fact that what people state as the causes of their resistance may have little to do with its real causes. For example, an individual may state that she is opposed to a decentralization because it will disrupt critical work processes. A little probing may reveal that she is really worried about being able to perform her new responsibilities at an acceptable level, namely, to be revealed as less competent than required. Probing resistance will also provide an opportunity to ask resisters for their suggestions related to the change effort, thus giving them an opportunity to work towards the change objective rather than against it.

The next step in Karp's approach is to develop an *agreement about actions* to be taken by both or either of the parties in order to reduce the level of resistance to the proposed change. This step is essential because it provides closure to the issue and ensures that no agreement will be forgotten.

Karp emphasizes that the objective of his approach is not to eliminate all resistance, because it is not possible to do so. Instead, it is to work with and reduce needless resistance.

KURT LEWIN, THE FATHER OF MODERN CHANGE THEORY

No discussion of organizational change would be complete without a brief discussion of Kurt Lewin and his thoughts about change. Lewin died in 1947, but many of his students and followers have become widely recognized as leaders in facilitating planned organizational and social change. One of Lewin's most important contributions to change management theory was his concept of 'force-field analysis', which is one of the most powerful techniques available today for examining and dealing with the processes and dynamics of intentional personal or organizational change.

Lewin pointed out that any complex change situation can be defined and analysed as a 'force-field' in which multiple forces are interacting. Some of these forces are acting in support of the change effort while others are operating in opposition. That is, there are both 'driving' and 'restraining' forces operating in every change effort. Driving forces create pressure that attempts to push the *current state* in the direction of some set of preferred conditions or *desired state*, that is, they act in support of change. Restraining forces generate pressures that work to maintain the *current state* against change and therefore act to hinder achievement of the desired state (see Figure 9.1).

When there is a gap between the current and desired state in an organization, a

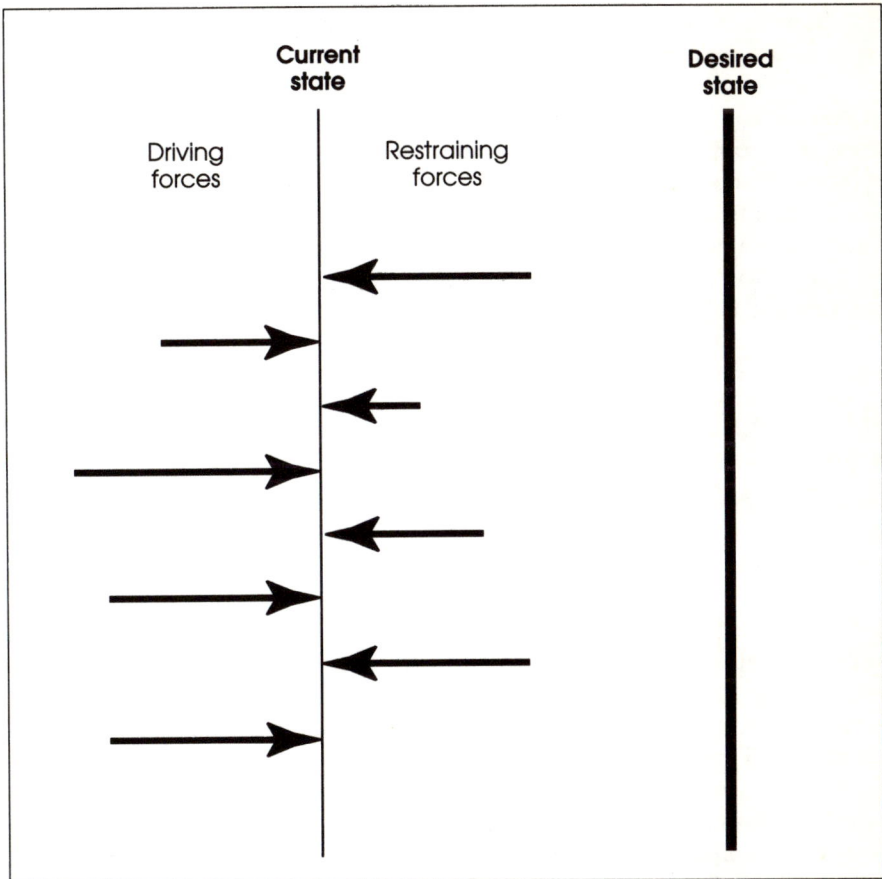

FIGURE 9.1   Kurt Lewin's force-field

certain amount of tension is generated; the larger the gap, the greater the tension. However, the mere existence of this tension is not enough to cause change. Lewin observed that regardless of the size of the gap between a current and desired state, a situation will remain 'stable' as long as the sum of the power of the driving forces more or less equals the sum of the power of the restraining forces. Conversely, a situation will only change when the sum of the power of the driving and restraining forces are rearranged and made unequal. If the driving forces become greater than the restraining forces, change will occur in the direction of the desired state. If restraining forces are greater, the current state is likely to be pushed farther from the desired state and the size of the gap will be increased.

An analysis of the force-field for any given change situation sets the stage for determining what strategies might be most appropriate in order to reduce the gap and thereby reduce the amount of tension within the organization. If we could somehow measure the 'power' of driving and restraining forces in kilograms we might find that the sum of the energy contained in all of the driving forces equalled, say, 100 kg of pressure. We might also find that the sum of the energy in all restraining forces also equalled 100 kg. With 100 kg of pressure driving towards the objective (the desired state) and 100 kg of pressure pushing in the opposite direction there would be a total of 200 kg of pressure operating in the current state field or situation and, because the driving and restraining forces are equal, there would be no change in the situation (see Figure 9.2).

In order to change a situation in equilibrium we must create an *imbalance* between the driving and restraining forces. There are two major strategies for attempting to create a disruptive imbalance between driving and restraining forces and thereby moving the current state in the direction of the desired state: (1) increasing the power or number of driving forces or (2) decreasing the power or number of restraining forces.

Increase the power or number of driving forces: The most frequently used strategy for change is to increase the strength or number of the driving forces. Using our 200 kg example, the power of driving forces can be increased to 125 kg by adding a new 25 kg force or by increasing an existing force by 25 kg. The assumption of this strategy is that 125 kg of driving forces acting against 100 kg of restraining forces will cause the situation to change in the desired direction. However, what usually happens when you increase pressure exerted by driving forces is that it tends to induce the creation of new and/or more powerful restraining forces in an effort to hold the current state in its present position. A 25 kg increase in driving forces is likely to be countered with an increase in restraining forces by 25 kg (or more). As illustrated in Figure 9.3, if a 25 kg increase in driving forces is countered by a 30 kg increase in restraining forces this is likely to move the current state away from the desired state. More importantly, increasing the pressure in the system from the 200 kg equilibrium level to a total pressure of 255 kg is likely to create enough heat and friction to overload the system.

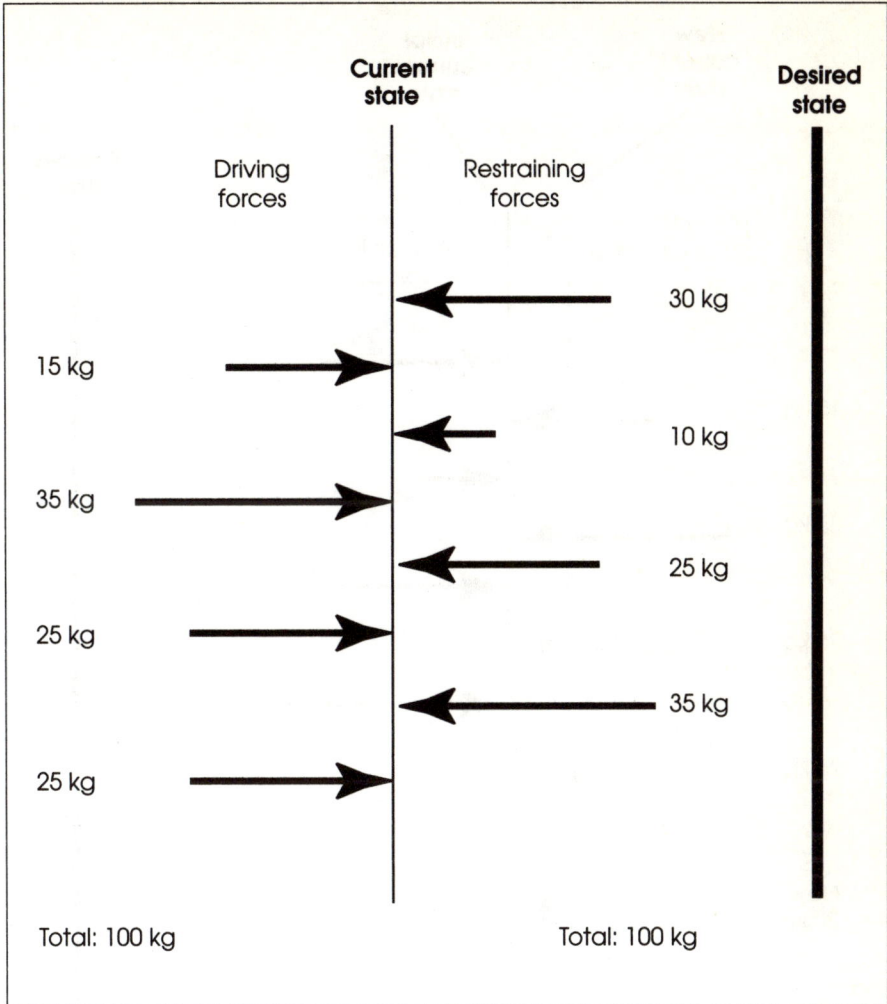

FIGURE 9.2   Driving and restraining forces in equilibrium

As restraining forces build up, the overall pressure on the system is further increased, putting the system in danger of being overloaded.

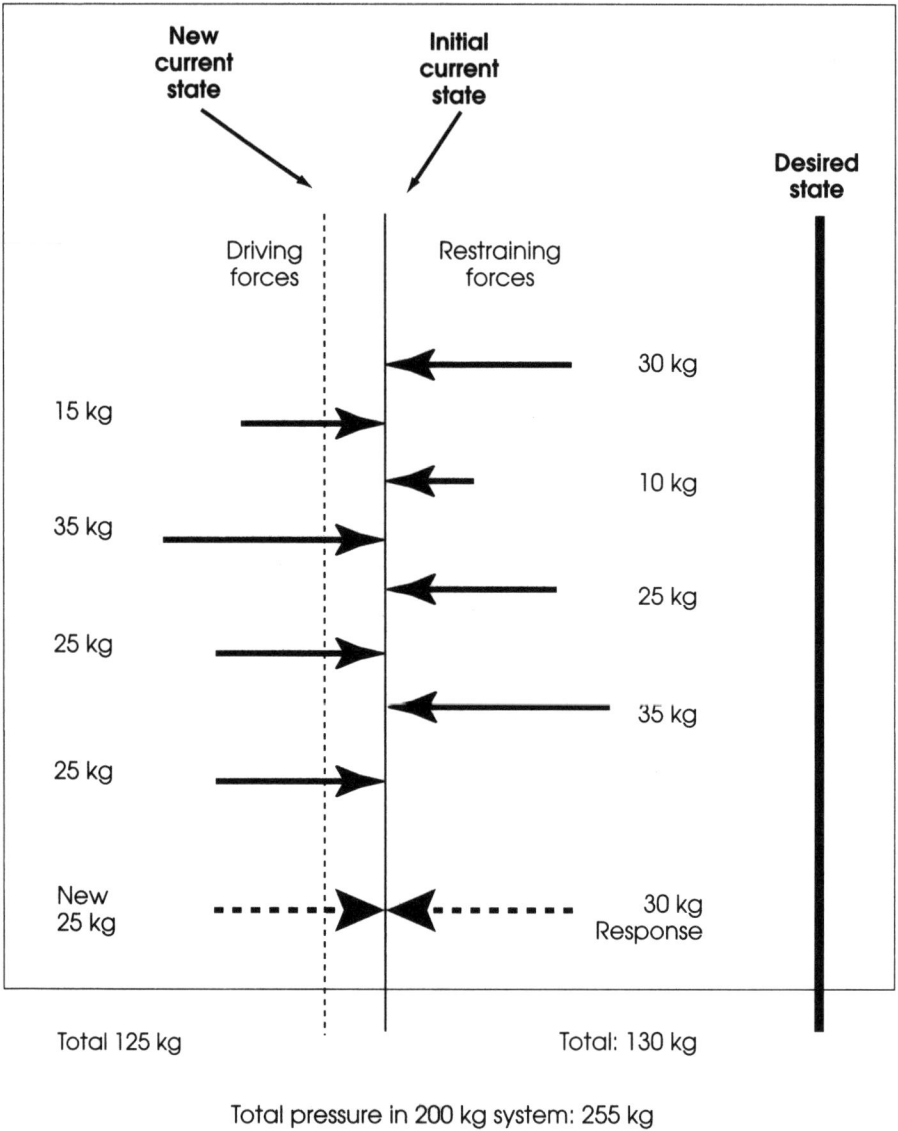

FIGURE 9.3   The likely result of increasing driving forces

Case in point

One of the authors was asked to facilitate a two-day seminar for the Regional Marketing Managers for a major airline. The intended topic of this seminar was 'Effective People Management Skills'. The Vice President of Marketing opened the seminar with the following: 'Ladies and gentlemen, as you all know, I have been with this company for a little over six months. During that time I have had ample opportunity to observe your skills as managers and have come to the conclusion that most of you would not even qualify as supervisors with my previous employer. Therefore, I have brought in Dr Zackrison to give you a brief introduction to professional management; a topic unfamiliar to most of you!'

Regional Managers' reaction was to sit back in their chairs with their arms crossed tightly over their chests. It did not take an expert in body language to read their message: 'Come on Doc; we dare you to teach us about anything!' After a half-day of trying futilely to reach the Regional Managers, the author was forced to give up. However, before leaving the premises he gave the Marketing Vice President a short, but very concise private lecture on the importance of handling co-workers with respect.

The Marketing Vice President in the above case attempted to reduce the gap between the current and desired states by increasing driving forces (using a hammer!). The result was that a group of senior managers who would, in normal circumstances, have welcomed new ideas and skills, became totally non-receptive. The only positive result of his tactic was that the Marketing Vice President was replaced not long after the seminar.

Decrease the power or number of restraining forces: A second strategy for destabilizing the balance between driving and restraining forces is to eliminate or reduce the strength of one or more existing restraints. As illustrated in Figure 9.4, if the power of restraining forces is reduced by 25 kg we would still have the original 100 kg of pressure from driving forces but only 75 kg of pressure from restraining forces. This strategy would result in the current state moving in the direction of the desired state while simultaneously reducing the total pressure on the system to 175 kg. This, in turn, results in less friction, less heat and less chance of a systemic breakdown during the change process.

Clearly, the preferred strategy for inducing planned change in most situations is to seek ways to reduce the restraining forces, rather than (automatically) increasing the driving forces. There is, however, a third strategy for reducing the gap between a current and a desired state and that is to move the desired state in the direction of your current state. Admittedly, this strategy often means admitting

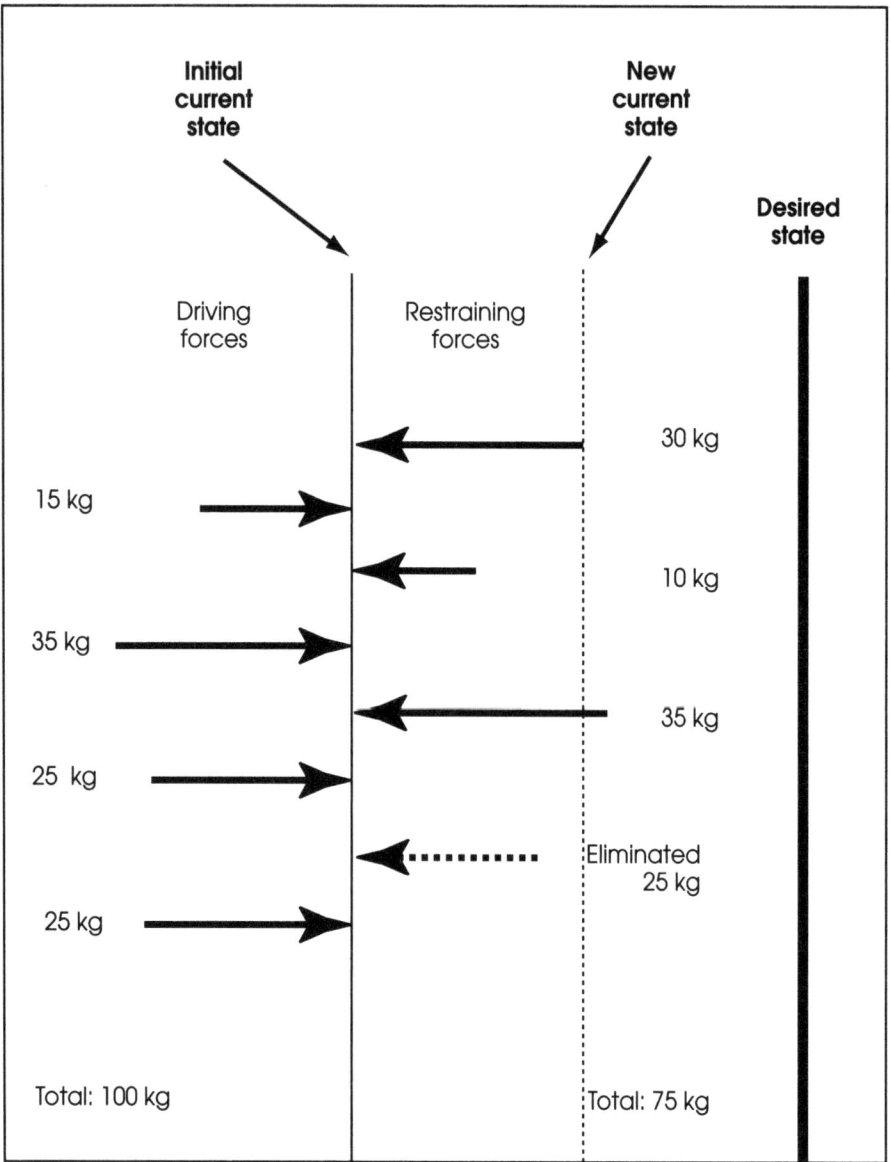

Total pressure in 200 kg system: 175 kg

FIGURE 9.4   The likely result of decreasing restraining forces

defeat, but that may be a very realistic choice when the only other alternative is banging your head against a stone wall in a futile effort to attain impossible goals. This strategy should only be used in situations in which (1) critical restraining forces are immutable, that is, they are either beyond your control or ability to influence positively, and/or (2) you are unwilling to accept the negative consequences of increasing the driving forces.

Before leaving Lewin we would like to share his metaphor for how to stimulate change with a minimum of resistance. Assume that you want to change the shape of a standard ice cube to a form that resembles a golfball, without reducing the volume of ice. One method would be to chip off the corners and file down the rough edges until the piece of ice was in the proper form. Unfortunately, that tactic would result in the loss of a great deal of the ice cube's volume. Another approach would be to attempt to force the ice cube into a round mould. The likely result of this approach would be that either the ice cube or the mould would break under the pressure. Both of the preceding approaches involve manipulating the driving forces, and both are doomed to failure. Lewin suggests that one of the forces restraining the reshaping of the ice cube is the fact that it is currently in a solid form. His recommended approach would be to first thaw the ice cube and then pour the water into the round form, which should then be refrozen. Strategies that attempt to create change by increasing the power and/or number of driving forces usually have some of the same consequences as trying to chip, file or cram an ice cube into a round form. A natural reaction to such strategies is a corresponding increase in restraining forces and the ultimate failure of the planned change effort.

A FORMULA FOR SUCCESSFUL CHANGE EFFORTS

Once you have determined that organizational change is necessary, you will need a roadmap that will guide you and your consultant through the change process. The roadmap that we prefer is a change formula that we have expanded on from the ideas of David Gleicher and Dick Beckhard. This change formula focuses attention on four factors that are inherent in any attempt to generate change. Each of these factors must be effectively managed if the change effort is to be successful. Our change formula, written mathematically, is:

$$SCE = D \times V \times S_{fs} \times B$$

SCE REPRESENTS THE CHANCES OF SUCCEEDING WITH A CHANGE EFFORT

The letters *SCE* in the change formula stand for the likelihood that the change effort will achieve the goals and objectives for which it was initiated. It is placed to the left of the equals sign to indicate that the chances of success of a change effort are dependent on the four factors that follow.

D REPRESENTS *D*ISSATISFACTION

The *D* in the change formula represents the degree to which you and other significant members of your organization are Dissatisfied with the current state. The primary motivation for any change effort is derived from dissatisfaction. Dissatisfaction is a major source of energy that can provide the power to let go, shift gears, experiment, discover, learn, persist and adapt to changing conditions. If there is no dissatisfaction, there is likely to be little or no change. However, senior management dissatisfaction alone is seldom sufficient to ensure the success of a change effort. It is equally important that anyone who is, or believes they are, impacted by the change effort or who is responsible for implementing any significant aspect of the change effort also feels a sense of dissatisfaction with the current state.

Anyone with teenage children will immediately recognize the importance of the above distinction. Teenagers won't willingly change simply because their parents are dissatisfied with their behaviour or appearance. In fact, the surest way to guarantee that they will resist changing is for the change to be suggested by their parents! Teenagers will willingly change their behaviour or appearance when, and only when, they, too, are dissatisfied with it. The same is true in organizations. People will accept and support change because they, personally, see, understand and feel the need to change. They will not accept or support a change simply because the organization's CEO has ordered it.

V REPRESENTS *V*ISION

The *V* in the change formula represents the degree to which the change effort is focused on achieving a clear, mutually understood and accepted desired state or Vision. As Alice was wandering around in Wonderland, she was faced with a fork in the road and asked the Cheshire Cat which road she should take. Upon finding that Alice didn't know where she wanted to go, the Cheshire Cat replied that it made no difference which road Alice chose. The same is true of organizations; unless you have a clear vision of where you want your change effort to take you, it will make little difference which road you take!

As with Dissatisfaction, it is important that a critical mass of organizational members share, accept and support a commonly understood Vision for the change effort. Again, this means that those impacted by or involved in implementing key aspects of the change effort need to understand and accept the vision, goals and objectives for that effort.

S REPRESENTS STRATEGY, *fs* REPRESENTS *f*IRST *s*TEPS

The *S* in the change formula is a measure of the degree to which the change effort is guided by a Strategy for moving from the current state (Dissatisfaction) to the desired state (Vision). The suffix *fs* infers that the most essential components of any change strategy are the first steps. Two common mistakes made by senior managers as they plan a change effort are: (1) failure to change their strategy when necessary, and (2) failure to implement the first step in time.

Failure to change their strategy when necessary

Many managers and consultants live by the rule: 'Plan your work; work your plan'. Once a plan has been agreed upon, they implement it in a way that resembles racehorses with blinkers; they run straight for the finish line and refuse to be distracted by things that might interfere with their predetermined course, even when these 'distractions' might make the difference between winning and losing the race! Most major change efforts require complex strategies that are meant to be implemented over months and even years, and many things can change during that time. In fact, in over 50 years of combined consulting experience, neither of the authors of this book can recall seeing a successful change effort that was implemented as originally planned. Without exception, they all required significant modification which, in some cases, meant scrapping the original strategy completely.

Failure to take the first step in time

You are no doubt familiar with cautious organization leaders who are reluctant to implement a strategy until it is 'complete', which, for them, means that every step, from start to finish, must be meticulously timed, costed and resource loaded. Such leaders are often very conscientious, conservative people who are vitally concerned with making prudent decisions. They can serve as important reality checks and restrain overly enthusiastic visionaries from prematurely committing the organization to exorbitant risks. Unfortunately, such overly cautious leaders often fail to recognize that their search for a 'perfect plan' may not be worth the benefits that they expect, especially since it is almost certain that any long-term complex plan will need to be significantly changed and adjusted anyway.

Because it is not possible to create perfect strategies that cover the duration of broad scope organizational changes, we personally prefer a 'just enough' approach to strategic planning processes. That is, any long-term strategic planning that we do, for ourselves or with our clients, becomes 'looser' as the initial planning process proceeds:

1. We are extremely strict in our demand that the strategic planning process begins with a clearly defined, mutually agreed vision or desired state to which all members of the planning team are committed.
2. We are equally strict in our demand that the vision and desired state be defined in terms of concise, measurable goals. Whenever possible, we insist that these goals be defined in terms of the gap between the current and desired state. For example, to avoid such ambiguous goals as

'increase production', we push for more concrete goals such as 'to increase production from the current 25,000 widgets/day to 35,000/day without increasing current per unit production costs'.

3. We also demand that the overall goals for the project be divided into specific mileposts and that concrete, measurable time-bounded objectives be formulated for each milepost.

4. Next, is development of an overview of the resources that are likely to be required for each step of the project so that total project costs can be estimated.

5. Then, the first few significant steps of the strategy are completed in detail and the implementation phase is begun.

6. Finally, a plan is developed for when, how and by whom the remainder of the strategy is to be developed. This includes agreeing to specific procedures for capturing data from current steps and actions that may be of value in the formulation and/or implementation of future steps.

This approach enables us and our clients to identify, be more responsive to and deal more effectively with the unpredictable events that almost always emerge during a change effort.

B REPRESENTS *B*ELIEF

The *B* in the change formula is a measure of the degree to which key members of your organization believe in the likelihood that the change effort will produce the desired results. Large-scale organizational change is nothing new to the leaders and members of most organizations. They have gone through it several times in their professional lives and, unfortunately, many of them have learned that the changes they have experienced seldom live up to their pre-show publicity. As a result, many respond pessimistically, or even cynically, to any announced change within their organization. Simply stated, they do not believe that the change effort will make any real difference and, as a result, are usually poorly motivated to commit time and energy towards its implementation.

THE CHANGE FORMULA IN PRACTICE

If you view the change formula ($SCE = D \times V \times S_{fs} \times B$) in mathematical terms, *if any one of the elements in the formula is 'zero', the likelihood that the change effort will succeed is also 'zero'.*

DISSATISFACTION = 0

One of the authors was recently requested to design and implement a management training programme for a medium sized-company. The Managing Director and his senior executives had personally prepared a long list of 'competencies' that they believed their subordinate managers lacked and/or in which they were weak. As the first step in the assignment the consultant interviewed a number of the organization's managers. The majority of them defiantly asserted that they were already skilled in the specified competencies. Several managers suggested that the competencies were not relevant for their particular areas of responsibility. In general, they all thought that they were already doing a good job of managing. The only thing they were dissatisfied with was that 'senior management keeps trying to send us on courses instead of letting us do our jobs'.

The managers' reactions in the above example did not mean that they did not need the management training offered. Their reactions simply suggest that they did not personally *see* or *feel* that need. Their lack of dissatisfaction gave the leaders of the organization and their consultant three options:

First, *attempt to force feed the training*, recognizing that the more they press, the more resistance they will encounter from the prospective participants (as with Lewin's force-field). Even if the managers were forced to attend the prescribed training programme, they probably would not learn. If any of them did learn something, they probably would not apply, or would be prevented from applying, their learning to their jobs.

Second, *forget the whole thing*, which could be an extremely irresponsible decision if, in fact, their managers' skills were below an acceptable functional level. Under such circumstances, insufficiently competent middle managers would have successfully stopped senior management from bringing their managerial skills up to a minimum acceptable level, which could endanger the organization's long-term survival.

Third, *start afresh* by providing the targeted managers with an opportunity to discover, for themselves, that they can benefit from training designed specifically to improve their performance in the defined competencies.

VISION = 0

The senior management committee of a major governmental agency announced a decision to restructure the organization. Their formal announcement stated, 'we have decided to decentralize the organization in order to (1) reduce the number of decision-making levels and (2) place authority and responsibility closer to the actual work being done'. When asked, the majority of the middle managers within this organization stated that they believed the 'true' purpose of the decentralization was to (1) cut costs by reducing the number of middle managers by 20 per cent, and (2) get more work out of existing middle managers, supervisors and workers. As a result of these competing perceptions and beliefs about the ultimate purposes of the change effort, the organization's middle managers actively resisted decentralization. The three primary reasons for their reactions were the following.

First, that *management had, in fact, lied*. One of the primary reasons for decentralizing was, indeed, to cut costs, especially those costs associated with far too many middle managers located in a top heavy, bureaucratic central administration. Because middle managers were well aware that their superiors were lying, their trust in them was severely reduced.

Second, *individual senior managers clearly demonstrated that they had very different Visions for the change effort*. Middle managers quickly discovered that they would get a different vision of the change effort depending on which of their executives they talked to. One senior manager actually violated management committee confidentiality by stating to his subordinates that 'there will be no real changes; we just want to get rid of some of the dead wood'. Another told her employees that there would be no personnel cuts in her department. Two weeks later three of this executive's middle managers were declared redundant and given early retirement packages.

Third, *senior management, as a group, had not involved other members of the organization in a process of creating a common Vision for the new decentralized structure*. It is interesting to note that most of the middle managers in this organization shared senior management's views related to excessive administrative costs, dead wood, excessive levels of decision making, and so on. Had middle managers been invited to participate in creating the new vision, it is unlikely that the end result would have differed significantly from the vision created by the senior management committee. The only difference is that they would have been far more likely to have supported the change instead of resisting it.

All too often we find senior managers in an organization working at cross-purposes, each pursuing a personal version of the Vision for a change effort that favours their own division, department, region, product or business unit at the expense of others. We have little doubt that you are all too familiar with the competition and conflicts that this can create throughout your organization, especially when the individuals or groups involved start playing win–lose games with one another. When this happens in conjunction with a major change effort, the effects are often deadly.

We are also all too familiar with situations in which a consultant's vision for a change effort differs drastically from the vision held by the client. At times the difference is created consciously by the consultant who misrepresents or exaggerates the results that can be expected. At times the difference is created because the client and the consultant have not fully explored and agreed on the results that can be expected. Whatever the cause, the results are the same; the client learns to distrust consultants.

STRATEGY, INCLUDING FIRST STEPS = 0

A large government agency spent over two years developing a strategy for implementing a new organizational structure. During that time numerous study groups, project teams and task forces were formed. Each of these groups did their work and submitted their reports and then waited for something to happen, but nothing did. By the time the strategy was complete, a large number of the agency's best managers had found jobs elsewhere; conflicts between individuals, groups, sections and departments were rampant; productivity was at an all time low; and the number of complaints from the organization's customers had increased drastically. One of the most serious consequences of the delay was that once the strategy was finally complete, things had changed so much within the organization that it was no longer applicable or relevant.

A well formulated strategy may not be enough to guarantee the successful implementation of that strategy. As with the previous elements of the change formula, it is essential to ensure that all key members and groups within the organization understand, accept and are committed to your strategy.

BELIEF = 0

One of the authors worked for four days with a senior management committee, helping them to plan for a major change in the organization's mission, direction and goals. At the end of the fourth day the team appeared to be in agreement on the causes of their dissatisfaction, their vision for the future of their organization, a strategic plan for reaching their desired future, and each team member's key responsibilities for implementing that plan. The workshop was concluded with a dinner during which wine was served, followed by cocktails. With his fifth martini in hand, the HR Director took the then 45 year old consultant to one side and said, 'Son, I have worked in this organization for thirty years. Every five years or so, some idiot decides to change things. As far as I know, none of these changes has ever done more than cause trouble and confusion for a few weeks, and then it's back to "business as usual". Why in hell should I put energy into a new change effort that is bound to fail? I'm retiring in three years!'

Here is a situation where a member of the senior management committee with a key role in communicating and supporting the change effort had no belief whatsoever in the success of that effort. As a result, it would have been highly unlikely that the change effort would have succeeded had he not been strongly and effectively encouraged to accept an early retirement package.

APPLYING THE CHANGE FORMULA

The first step in using the change formula is to conduct an early assessment to determine whether each element is strong enough to support the intended change. The results of this assessment can provide direct clues about where to direct your energy and resources:

○   **If D is low**, you will have to increase the level of dissatisfaction. Dissatisfaction can be 'awakened' by using employee questionnaires or focus group discussions to illuminate problem areas and to mobilize energy to deal with common concerns. Dissatisfaction can also be 'created' by clearly defining the negative consequences of continuing without change.

○   *If V is low*, you will have to mobilize formal and informal leaders to formulate and agree upon a mutually understood and mutually acceptable vision for the change effort; for example, they need to have a significant degree of agreement related to how things will be when the change effort is complete. More importantly, the vision must be attractive enough (or the consequences dire enough) that they are willing to commit their personal time, energy and resources into reaching it.

○   *If S_{fs} is low*, the best approach here might be to establish an initial track record of successes by selecting a subsystem within your organization and use it as a pilot or demonstration project that you can experiment with. For example, a pilot project might be limited to your senior management team, to the most effective subsystem in the organization, or to a subsystem that is 'hurting' and whose leaders and members are asking for help.

○   *If B is low*, you will need to commit time, energy and resources towards a campaign to convince organization members that you are serious about this change effort and that you fully intend to see that it achieves real, measurable results.

The preceding change formula is an excellent tool for screening consultants for a potential change effort. The consultant you hire must not only be fully aware of each of the four elements of the formula; s/he must also be competent to build clarity, consensus, ownership and commitment around each of the four components.

SUMMARY

We presented the preceding change management concepts and techniques in the context of helping you, as a senior manager, to evaluate the change management skills of external consultants that you are considering for specific assignments. As you do so, you will discover – if you haven't already done so – that most consultants know very little about the effective management of change.

The preceding discussion of change also indicates our bias that change management is not merely 'a part of' a manager's job – it *is* a manager's job. In fact, we find it quite difficult to identify anything that a manager should be doing that does not require the conscientious application of change management skills. That means that the concepts and techniques that we have presented in this chapter are not only relevant when you are considering engaging an external consultant – they should be a standard tool in your management tool kit.

PART IV
CHECKLISTS

❖

ONGOING CONSULTANT EVALUATION

Checklist IV.1
Level of results

The questions in this checklist are based on the following five levels of results from a consultant's efforts:

Level 1: Participants are *enjoying* the activity.

Level 2: Participants are *learning* the skills and/or concepts intended by the activity.

Level 3: Participants are *able to apply* their newly learned skills and/or concepts in the performance of their jobs.

Level 4: Participants are *allowed to apply* their newly learned skills and/or concepts in the performance of their jobs.

Level 5: The consultant's efforts are making *a real difference* in the effectiveness of our organization.

1. At which of the above levels should the consultant's results be visible thus far in the project?

2. At which of the above levels are the consultant's results visible thus far in the project?

3. Is there a gap between our responses to questions 1 and 2, and, if so, what is causing that gap?

4.   If the gap is positive, that is, actual results are exceeding our expectations, what can we learn from our success?

5.   If the gap is negative, that is, actual results fall short of our expectations, what can we do to change the situation?

Checklist IV.2
Keeping the effort on track

The following checklist can be used as part of an ongoing evaluation of a project to monitor its progress against predefined mileposts. We suggest the following three-point scale for this checklist:

3 = The effort is going **extremely well** in this area.
2 = Some **adjustment is needed** to improve performance in this area.
1 = **Major adjustments are needed** to improve performance in this area.

3 2 1   1. The project is unfolding as originally intended.

3 2 1   2. The project is producing the expected results.

3 2 1   3. The project is on schedule.

3 2 1   4. Our project planning and implementation processes have responded with appropriate flexibility to unexpected events or conditions.

3 2 1   5. We are well aware of and responding appropriately to unintended side-effects being created by this project.

3 2 1   6. We are getting what we expect from our consultant.

3 2 1   7. The members of our organization are gaining knowledge, skills, and insights as the result of our consultant's contributions.

3 2 1   8. The members of our organization have made positive changes in their behaviour and/or attitudes as the result of our consultant's contributions.

3 2 1   9. The members of our organization are responding well to our consultant and his/her contributions.

3 2 1 10. We have developed a productive, effective relationship with our consultant.

3 2 1 11. Our consultant has an appropriate level of influence over the management and members of our organization – neither too little nor too much.

3 2 1 12. Our consultant is using appropriate, acceptable methods, techniques and activities in his/her consultant efforts.

3 2 1 13. Our consultant demonstrates an understanding of and appropriate respect for our organization's culture, including its norms and taboos.

3 2 1 14. Our consultant maintains his/her focus on the specific task, problem and/or issues for which s/he was engaged.

3 2 1 15. Our consultant is receptive to relevant but previously hidden issues that might require him/her to modify the focus of the project in an appropriate and useful manner.

3 2 1 16. Our consultant has actively sought ways to appropriately involve the members of our organization in the consulting project.

3 2 1 17. Our consultant has maintained a 'helicopter' perspective.

Checklist IV.3
Evaluating the likelihood that your change effort will succeed

The following checklist can be used to determine the degree to which your intended change effort is likely to succeed – or fail. The scale we recommend for this checklist is as follows:

3 = We are **strong** in this area.
2 = We **need to improve** in this area.
1 = We are **weak** in this area.

3 2 1   1. Our senior executives and managers understand the importance of dealing positively with resistance to change and are prepared to respond appropriately.

3 2 1   2. We have conducted a force-field analysis of our problem and have a clear picture of our current state, desired state, driving forces and restraining forces.

3 2 1   3. Our senior executives and managers understand the importance of reducing restraining forces as opposed to increasing driving forces and are prepared to respond appropriately.

3 2 1   4. Dissatisfaction with the current state is high among those attempting to initiate this change effort.

3 2 1   5. Dissatisfaction with the current state is high among those responsible for implementing and/or impacted by this change effort.

3 2 1   6. The individuals attempting to initiate this change effort have a clear, commonly held vision of how our situation should be at some point in the future.

3 2 1   7. Individuals responsible for implementing and/or impacted by this change effort understand, accept and trust the vision presented by those initiating the change effort.

3 2 1   8. A sufficiently detailed strategy has been prepared and agreed to and key members of our organization are committed to doing what is required for that strategy to succeed.

3 2 1   9. The individuals attempting to initiate this change effort have an honest, realistic belief in their chances of succeeding.

3 2 1   10. Individuals responsible for implementing and/or impacted by this change effort believe that the change effort will succeed.

INDEX

❖